MW01350424

GROWING COMES FROM PLANTING SEEDS

A Roadmap for Mentoring, Coaching, and Developing Relationships that will Last a Lifetime

Ron Emery

TABLE OF CONTENTS

Dedication

I would like to dedicate this book to my family, who keeps putting up with me through all my flaws. My wife, who allows countless hours of research and writing in the evenings, my daughter, whom I keep referring to in this book as an example exposing our relationship for the world to see, my son, whom I don't refer to very often because if you could see him, he would probably be rolling his eyes right now--he got that from me, and my good friend, Steve, who helped tremendously with the cover, as well as laying this out for content. I would like to thank the countless others, who over the years have provided their own mentorship to me in this book. Without all of the help from the above, this book never would have been possible. I hope you enjoy reading this as much as I enjoyed writing it.

Chapter One:

Mentoring and Coaching

You will notice that this book is laid out to provide you with wide margins and spaced-out content. I want you to use this as a workbook above all. Feel free to make notes to yourself in the margins, dog-ear the pages, and use your highlighters wherever and whenever you can. The best way to learn is through trial and error, so keep your notes and make yourself utilize this as a handbook for your path to improvement and ultimately to fulfillment. That is what life is all about after all, isn't it? Try the suggested exercises and keep track of your results. Jot down the ideas you have regarding your mentoring and personal relationships as you read this. Because, after all, aren't we all looking for ways to feel good about ourselves by helping others? That is why we give our old cars and clothes to help the less fortunate. That is why we volunteer at the local soup kitchen, not just to help the less fortunate, but for us to feel good about ourselves as well, to make sure the world that we have taken so much from gets a little back. So use the book as it is meant, and keep it for a long time. Use the knowledge contained inside of it to help make yourself a better person, as well as to give back to others to help them improve.

As I have travelled throughout the years, certain things keep happening and coming back to me, and all of it is centered on my relationships with people. Years ago on “take your daughter to work day,” I had my daughter join me to get a taste of what the business world was like. At the end of the day she told me, “I figured out what I want to be when I grow up, Dad.” She went on to say, “I really don’t understand what you do, but I see you have friends all over the globe, and I want to do whatever you do, Dad.” Now, I hadn’t adequately explained what I did for a living, but she picked up on how connected I must have been to mentors, protégés*, coaches, and just general business associates. And by the way, I think that is great.

---

*My preferred term is “protégé,” and not “mentee.” I like the word protégé better because it emphasizes the relationship between the mentor and the protégé, focusing on how the mentor is a teacher and a friend, and showing how the relationship is a valuable one for both parties. Mentee, to me, feels like it’s purely a business term. When my sources use mentee, though, I’ll stick with what they write.

I have always believed in the school of hard knocks. I believe in a couple of other business tenets very strongly, too. First, I believe that you learn more from witnessing the actions of others and emulating them than you will ever read in a book. (Provided that they are good examples, of course.) There's no substitute for real world experience. Second, I believe you learn more by doing and applying what you learn in your own test laboratory. I believe that you, through trial and error, test your theories and find out just what works for you in all cases. Just because it doesn't work for your neighbor, doesn't mean it won't work for you. Most things in life aren't cut and dried.

The stories I will tell you in this book are all things that have happened when I have applied just what I have learned, and I will tell you when they have worked and just when they have backfired. Keep in mind, this knowledge or success didn't happen overnight, and it won't happen overnight for you, but if you truly embrace what mentoring, coaching, and developing business relationships are, it will truly fulfill and reward you. I know this from experience because I have been rewarded through my relationships with others, not just monetarily, but spiritually, too, and hopefully you will get a good sense of that as well.

One of the young men I mentored years ago and I were sitting having a cup of coffee and he commented that he wished he could do something for me for all of the help I had given him. I said, "Don't worry; someday I may be working for you, instead of you working for me." It sounds farfetched, but it's not really. You see, it's funny what life holds in store for you. Years later, he turned me on to a project and got me an interview with the company he was working for, so it does happen. Business relationships throughout my career have a habit of resurrecting themselves. Maybe you go five or six years without speaking to someone, but you suddenly stumble across a project or a need and you happen to make that call to reconnect. And believe me, you do reconnect just right where you left off, because you had a trusting relationship back then and it can still be rekindled. But again, none of this will happen unless there is a trusting relationship built from mutual respect to begin with.

I decided to write about mentoring because I felt that even though there have been a number of articles written on the subject, there were no handbooks on how to mentor, certainly no solid comparisons between what the difference is between a mentor and a coach, and nothing on how to develop solid business relationships that I considered worthwhile, either. In fact, in many cases, mentoring and coaching are referred to as being synonymous, which in my experience they are not—they are very different efforts. They all have their place in today's world and really are different relationships, so maybe if we understood them a little better we can use that knowledge to our advantage. The traditional business relationship is sometimes taken for granted as well. There seems to be much focus on partnerships these days, which really aren't partnerships at all and, if you ask me, are pretty one-sided relationships at that. So how do you make all of this work? That question is why I took the time to pen some of my ideas and assemble them into this book.

When I started to think about a title for the book, I settled on *Growing Comes from Planting Seeds*. "Why?" You might ask. Well, it seems the older I get, the more I realize success in life is all about the knowledge you accumulate, and the thirstier I am for that knowledge. I just love to pick knowledge and pass it on to individuals and see what becomes of it. The "growing" part refers to my belief that we always need to be in a state of growth. If we are not in a state of growth, we begin to die. So challenge yourself to always learn, find something new to do every day, and listen to others to open your senses about what the world really is and how you can make it a little better place for all of us to live.

I like to play racquetball. The reason I like to play is I take unsuspecting participants and put them into my laboratory. I get to test their reaction to stress and their performance under stress. I get to test their resolve and patience as well as their temperament. I get a good sense of just how they react under various stimuli that I personally put them in. Yes, I am like the *mad scientist* of the racquetball court. Playing racquetball allows me to put an individual under all those parameters and see how they respond. I suppose you could do the same with any sport, really. Competition tells you a lot about the individual. Racquetball is not a team sport, unless you play doubles or cutthroat—it is an individual sport and it tells you a lot about the individual.

I think life is all about growing, and *continuing* to grow and develop. If we aren't learning, we are standing still and becoming complacent. I don't like that. If life is all about growing, how does the growing start? I think it is all about how we plant seeds. During my life I have planted so many seeds I have become a farmer (and oh yes, there is a chapter in this book about farming). But the farming I do is individual farming. I'm concerned with asking how we create better human beings. How do we make people more compassionate about what they do, and how do we make them do it with repeatability and improvement every time? How do we get them excited about the tasks at hand?

That's why I think mentoring is so cool. You get to influence someone else with your actions, advice, and counsel, and you have to do it with trust. Coaching principles are very similar to the principles for building long lasting business relationships. Trust turns out to be the common thread in all of this, whether it is mentoring, coaching, or really any type of relationship. If there is no trust, the relationship always seems to suffer. I cannot emphasize enough the importance of trust. Trust is the foundation every relationship is based on. Your partner in a trusting relationship needs to realize that you hold the relationship in such high esteem that you would never risk or question the trust in that relationship.

Many a friend has told me that I have a gift when it comes to engaging with people and getting them interested in following me. So I figured there must be something to it. A few years ago I invited a friend from Toronto to my condo in Michigan to see a U of M game. He brought another friend with him. His friend, Justin, asked me during breakfast the next day if I felt I had a higher calling. That is a surprise comment, isn't it? After a few-minute discussion on just what he meant, he described to me that he felt he was on a much lower plane than I was and that I had a unique perspective on life and also relationships. He explained he could sense how I engaged with people, and then involved them in the conversation, making them comfortable and trusting so they would actually listen to my advice. Pretty cool stuff to hear from a young man the age of my son. I thought to myself, was he onto something? Maybe something I hadn't quite figured out yet?

I had lunch with a business associate today and we started talking about gifts. The ability to communicate, understand, and give of one's self is a gift from God. We talked about the fact that if you don't use the gifts you were given, it's actually a crime against society and humanity. What we actually meant is that it is a sin to be given something and not use it—isn't it? So we are all empowered with various gifts. Some can sew, some can labor with their hands, some are musicians, some are artists; some of us have vision and some of us don't, but we have other gifts, and yes, some of them haven't even been discovered yet, and well, you get my point. If we don't use the talents we have either been given or we have learned, we aren't doing ourselves or each other any good at all.

My ex-boss in Toronto told me one time that I was the most engaging person he had ever met. I thought that that was an excellent way to describe me, and I was very humbled by his comment. I think to be engaged or to have the ability to engage is a great thing. Engaging, in my definition, means completely understanding the person you are communicating with. And isn't that what we all seek…to be understood by others? But to be engaged, you first have to listen and seek to understand. That provides the common thread between two parties. These instances, and many more of which you will read in this book, got me thinking about my purpose and what actually fulfills me, and what can fulfill you as well.

Now, this isn't a religious book, but it is one of spiritualism and one of discovering just what kind of person you are or intend to be. Imagine how powerful of a dynamic we could create if we could harness those feelings and make them part of our everyday life. Imagine how fulfilling it might be to give back with every breath. That got me thinking about mentoring and what it takes to become a mentor to someone. It got me thinking of being able to offer advice to someone and have them take it as constructive criticism of the way they are acting or behaving, and how that might help them in their lives—if they can learn through my mistakes. It got me thinking about walls, and why some people put up their walls when the potential mentor is around, while some people completely take them down. It also got me started thinking about things that I didn't even know were learning experiences at the time, but looking back, were significant for my development. This is a time to be reflective about your life experiences and just how they shaped you into the person you have become—and oh, by the way, if you aren't happy with the person you've become, what will you do to change it?

This week two things happened to me that are significant, particularly with regard to writing this book. A good friend, Michael Ross—who I will quote later in this book—and I were talking about some joint research, and he happened to mention how God provides gifts to all of us and how we go against God's intent when we don't use the gifts He has provided to us. Think about it for a minute and remove God from the equation. We all will agree that individuals have gifts. So is it unreasonable to expect people to figure out how to use those gifts to their best advantage, and to assume that if they don't utilize them they are going against the laws of nature? Something to think about....

Secondly, I met another friend for coffee today and he told me the following: "You and I were sitting right over there six months ago when you asked about me about losing my job, and do you remember what you told me?" I said I did not remember, and he told me, "You said that this would be a learning experience for me, and that I should take this as a way of improving myself and use it as a point of reflection. Well, I did, and I became a better man for it." You see, we don't even realize all the times we touch another with our advice and with our counsel. We really only know when they tell us. But spiritual or not, becoming a mentor and having genuine concern about another individual and helping them navigate through life's ups and downs is rewarding in itself. Use your gifts wisely and give them away freely to those that deserve them.

Being a mentor requires more than just listening to your protégé. It requires a caring concern for him or her. It requires that the mentor be selfless and put him or herself in the protégé's shoes and see exactly what the protégé sees. That is a little difficult to ask of the mentor. Egos must disappear, because they have to put aside for the sake of the protégé. So the mentor is a special person. You see, mentors really don't care about themselves as much as they care about the protégé. Usually, the best mentors are the ones who have been through "the wringer," have experienced what the protégé is about to face, and can objectively offer advice. And they offer their friendship and guidance free of charge, because that is their way of giving.

I happened to run across this article in the December 23, 2014 edition of Forbes, entitled "Five Ways People kill their Career Potential" by David Sturt and Todd Nordstrom, and they ask about what is most important to business people:

> …the desire to advance intellectually and emotionally, to leave a legacy in an industry, to build strong relationships with people you work with, or to become someone better than you are today? Sure, money is important, but, what about the qualitative side of loving the job you have?

We talk today so much about adding value and needing to think in a certain way, but what about the value you bring to the relationship? This is advice and counsel the protégé can't get anywhere else.

Sturt and Nordstrom go on to say:

> Not long ago, Right Management, a subsidiary of the staffing firm Manpower Group, released a survey that revealed job dissatisfaction among North American workers. Of the 411 workers surveyed throughout the U.S. and Canada, nearly two-thirds said they were not happy at work. 19% said they were actually satisfied with their jobs. And, 16% responded by saying they were just "somewhat satisfied."

These are the people we're curious about. They could have everything—the position, the authority, the car, the house—their lives could seemingly be perfect, yet something is missing.

What is it that makes some people move up the ladder while others sit idle? Is it the corporate culture? Is it the boss? Is it the employee? How do we reverse that trend? How many of those people who successfully climbed that ladder have a mentor behind them, leading the way and making sure that they have the proper advice along the way? This knowledge has served me well over the years, and it can serve you, too, if you learn how to harness its energy. So, I hope you can sense the energy in which this book was written. I hope that after reading this, it empowers you to seek fulfillment in everything you do as well.

What about the Millennials?

I need to mention the Millennials, not necessarily because my daughter is one and has all the Millennial traits, but because if we don't try and think the way our new generation of future workers thinks, we will lose the battle and the war. Millennials think very differently, and we can probably learn a lot from them. We manage today thinking about Baby Boomers and Generation X, but don't Millennials have a very different way of looking at the same problems? (Remember they are what the future is going to look like, and we have to prepare our organizations for this upcoming group of workers.) How do Millennials look at mentoring and coaching? Do they have a sense of entitlement about it? How are we as an organization prepared to look at this in the future?

Karl Moore and Sienna Zampino, in an article for Forbes, entitled "The Modern Mentor in a Millennial Workplace," say that:

> Millennials have a bad reputation. They are seen as spoiled, lazy, and having high expectations. Put simply, they're considered immature, but we think otherwise. Based on our research, we believe that Boomers and Gen Xers have important roles to play in mentoring Millennials and helping them harness their valuable talent.

They say in their article that this new group of workers is more intent on finding mentors to help them navigate the waters of the workplace than previous generations who might have insisted on finding those pitfalls on their own. The managers of today need to embrace that within the new workforce and adapt. Moore and Zampino tell us that:

> Millennials acknowledge, albeit not out loud, that they have certain limitations. They are aware that they lack some crucial elements in order to move forward. They view mentors as meaningful contributors to their personal growth. Millennials consider them confidantes; wiser individuals who can provide guidance. At times, Millennials' topics of interest can be controversial, requiring feedback prior to official discussion. Annual salary increases, for example, are best addressed with prior consultation. Mentors serve as fountains of knowledge for these kinds of topics.
>
> When searching for mentors, Millennials do not limit themselves to their work settings. After all, they are active in many different forums, the world of LinkedIn, for example,

> which provides immediate access to industry professionals from around the world. In the case of Millennials, users are able to quickly connect and contact influential people. Don't be surprised if you notice that your LinkedIn profile is being viewed by unknown faces.

I, in fact, reach out to many younger people, simply because if I am looking to build a sustainable business, these are the leaders of tomorrow. Moore and Zampino go on to say, "Millennials are naturally curious. They want to learn more about your academic background and personal career path. Knowing this contributes to their overall understanding of how to move forward in a career." This is a very different way of learning and engaging than the previous generations. While researching information for this book, I ran across a very telling graph created by Jeanne C. Meister and Kalie Willyerd in *The Harvard Business Review*, entitled "Mentoring Millenials." They write:

Millennials often look at mentoring as a two-way street, an opportunity to learn as well as share exactly what they have learned through their advanced use of social media, as well as their view of today's marketplace, buyers, consumers and users of products. They look at this as their value-added contribution to the company that has hired them. They have expectations from their bosses that they will provide direction and a solid career path for them. They believe that the company they work for will provide them challenges and opportunities for them to learn and grow, while allowing them the opportunity to blend work with the rest of their lives. They also believe that they have the opportunity to learn and grow while developing skills that they know need honing and developing, while giving new concepts and ideas back to the organization. This provides the millennial with a two-way street of learning and support. They lack the industry-specific knowledge that the older workers' may have, but this is their opportunity to learn and grow.

In short, Millennials are well connected, multi-taskers, and very technologically savvy, which is what we all want on our teams—but remember, this comes with the caveats of having transparency (I have found this the most difficult trait for a business to have, especially in the corporate world), as well as instant gratification and rewards (remember, they grew up in the technology era, where everything is instant). They believe their career paths will be collaborative and they will be part of that plan, as well as have a work life balance that will give them other opportunities to pursue their dreams.

What Millennials Want

...from their boss

TOP FIVE CHARACTERISTICS MILLENNIALS WANT IN A BOSS

Will help me navigate my career path

Will give me straight feedback

Will mentor and coach me

Will sponsor me for formal development programs

Is comfortable with flexible schedules

...from their company

TOP FIVE CHARACTERISTICS MILLENNIALS WANT IN A COMPANY

Will develop my skills for the future

Has strong values

Offers customizable options in my benefits/reward package

Allows me to blend work with the rest of my life

Offers a clear career path

...to learn

TOP FIVE THINGS MILLENNIALS WANT TO LEARN

Technical skills in my area of expertise

Self-management and personal productivity

Leadership

Industry or functional knowledge

Creativity and innovation strategies

Millennials desire feedback and dialogue about how they might get better, and just because they were born in the information age doesn't necessarily mean they are up to speed with the world around them, as there are many options to consume their time. Remember when we used to read the newspaper? Today, how many of us do? Probably very few. Remember how we'd watch the evening news? Fewer do that today because social media gives us the little snippets of news we need on a minute-by-minute basis. This generation grew up with this technology at their fingertips. They seldom go into subjects in depth. We used to wonder at *USAToday* because it changed the way we wanted to see the news. We wanted to see it graphically, in color and very short snippets. Well, lo and behold, the news business has changed. Lord knows radio has followed suit as well. Millennials would just as soon text as talk on the phone. They don't have the need for personal touch, (one in which the buyer is coddled or made to feel important). I for one believe that this need has been lost in our modern society, and it is sad to see, but who knows if the next generation will revive the ability to communicate through voice and the written word—these things always evolve, and what one generation prides itself on might be cast off by the next. So, I say get ready for the ride, and hone your mentoring skills for the new work force— the Millennials.

The Mentor Matrix

The more thought I put into this project, the more I thought about developing the Mentor Matrix, which will put my writing in a form that will very easily tell the story of relationships. I look at mentoring very differently than most, I suppose. I consider it to be a key part of a successful career, successful parenting, and successful living as well. I have had mentors, as well as having been a mentor to others. I have been coached and been a coach to many in a professional organization, and I have certainly had very successful business relationships. I think it is very important to understand the differences between all of these relationships. They are very different, and so is the business relationship. The business relationship has to be cultivated as well, and requires certain processes in order to grow. And of course, it is highly important to understand when and where you might apply approaches to all of these things, whether in mentoring, coaching, or just in developing strong business relationships.

There are two key "buzzwords" in Human Resource Management today…"mentoring" and "coaching." What do they actually mean, and why are they beneficial to you today? Organizations look at these descriptive words very differently, but what do they actually mean? How do they differ? I gave a recent talk at one of the ISM (Institute for Supply Management) regional symposiums, addressing such technical subjects as recent "Trends in Transportation" and a "Guide to Mentoring and Coaching." Now, I thought the first subject would have far more participants than the second. I can't tell you exactly why; I just thought the mentoring and coaching talk would have fewer participants because it was more abstract science, dealing with the human side of business. I was surprised to see more folks were interested in mentoring and coaching than in the more technical session. I suppose it has to do with what I call "soft science," which is more intuitive than "hard science," which is more based on facts. I think sometimes it is far easier to accept the data-driven details than the one that requires more feelings. But mentoring and coaching is not hard science. You are dealing with human emotions and minds.

That being said, let's get on the path to discovering more about mentoring, coaching, and business relationships.

- We always need to be in a state of growth.

- Life is all about growing, and continuing to grow and develop.

- Mentoring ultimately comes down to how we can create better people.

- Trust is the foundation that every relationship is based on.

- To engage with people, we first have to listen and seek to understand.

- Being a mentor requires more than just listening to your protégé. It requires caring concern for him or her.

- Mentoring is key to a successful career, successful parenting, and successful living.

- Think about what you want out of a mentoring or coaching effort. Assume you are the protégé and you are being mentored. What would your expectations be? What are your boundaries, if any? What walls of yours would have to come down for this effort to really benefit you? Do you know yourself well enough, or is some more internal reflection necessary? What would the end goals have to be for you to consider the effort successful?

- Also, think about your skills. What do you have that might be of some value to another, and what could you give to others by mentoring them. What are you expectations in return?

Chapter Two:

Who or What is a Mentor?

A mentor is a person who can be a sounding board, someone of experience who can listen and help development, while not losing sight of reality. "Mentors should keep their protégés' feet grounded, and support and stretch them to succeed personally and professionally," says Debbee Dale in "How to Set up a Mentoring Scheme." I think that is a perfect description. It is slightly more than just business in the fact it is a selfless relationship on the side of the mentor. It is a giving of one's advice and counsel, and the mentor is not upset or hurt if the protégé chooses a different path. Mentoring does require a skill that is not necessarily in everyone's demeanor. Jealousy often gets in the way of mentorship and probably is the biggest reason these relationships fail. "Mentoring is an intentional, developmental relationship in which a more experienced and more knowledgeable person nurtures the professional and personal life of a less experienced, less knowledgeable person," according to Wayne Hart in "What is Mentoring?"

Hart also says:

> The primary focus of a mentor is development of an individual with an eye to organizational outcomes as well as personal outcomes; the capacity of the mentor to influence rests heavily on his or her ability to relate in a nonauthoritative way while, paradoxically, guiding the mentee or the protegé from the perspective of a superior position and expertise. (7)

Many of these relationships, which may start out in a professional way, really turn out to be close personal friendships as the relationship continues. Mentors must pull and push their protégés. Mentoring requires strength in two different but complementary behaviors. First, mentors must *lead* by guiding interaction with their protégés. Mentors invest themselves in their protégés and uplift them, providing not only support, but empowerment. Secondly, Mentors must *support* protégés. Mentors push their protégés to become their best by encouraging development in areas of expressed need in their inventory. The protégé actually responds by not wanting to disappoint the mentor, which helps the protégé mature immensely. Mentoring is a spontaneous endeavor and in most cases cannot be planned, as the activity of coaching can. A document from Baylor University's Mentoring for Adolescent Development, entitled "Stages of a Mentoring Relationship," states that the mentoring relationship evolves over time and according to four distinct stages when a formal mentoring program is in place:

> ***Stage 1***
>
> The mentor and the protégé become acquainted and informally clarify their common interests, shared values, and future goals and dreams. If taking the time to become acquainted with one another, interests, values, and goals become a high priority, and the relationship seems to get off to a better start. In this stage, there may be a lack of communication, or difficulty in communicating. Protégés may be reluctant to trust mentors, and may even attempt to manipulate them. The relationship may

remain in this stage from one to six meetings. In the professional world, individuals who have become mentors have analyzed aspiring newcomers in their field and have selected promising young protégés to nurture. Most of these relationships work out very well. Even though the commonalities between the mentor and the protégé in a community mentoring setting may be less than that of a mentoring pair in a business setting, the methods of mentoring remain similar. Mentors must be careful not to allow their preconceptions to dictate how they will approach the relationship and define who they think the protégé should become.

While charting a course for her approach to the relationship, the mentor must consider three factors:

- The relative eagerness the protégé brings to this relationship.
- The similarities in personal styles (animated, low-key;

spontaneous, reflective; gentle, harsh; reticent, boisterous).

• The similarities in expected short- and long-term goals.

Stage 2

The mentor and protégé communicate initial expectations and agree upon some common procedures and expectations as a starting point. In the less likely event that the two individuals may not be compatible, the pair is able to part on a friendly basis. In Stage 2, there will be more listening, sharing, and confiding in one another. Values will be compared, and personal concerns will be expressed. During this stage, the mentor will likely be introduced to the protégés family. The relationship may remain in this stage from one to three months.

Stage 3

The mentor and the protégé begin to accomplish the actual purposes of mentoring. Gradually, needs become fulfilled, objectives are met, and intrinsic growth takes place. New challenges are presented and achieved. Stage 3 is the stage of acceptance, but it is also a stage of change, where a protégé is more likely to exercise self-discipline.

Stage 4

The mentor and the protégé close their mentoring association and redefine their relationship. Follow-up is conducted. In summary, in the four stages the mentor and protégé will acquaint themselves with one another, determine values and goals, achieve those goals, and close their relationship."

But remember, mentoring programs are not always official, and they don't necessarily follow the above rules. In many cases a mentoring relationship just happens. You will often hear me say (and I will probably say it a few times in this book) that when the student is ready, the teacher will appear. That is what happens in a lot of mentoring cases. The mentor and the protégé just happen to find each other and the relationship is developed. There have been many cases in my life where the relationships just happen to work between myself and the protégé and develop into a significant mentoring relationship, and that relationship goes on to last a period of time, or even a lifetime. There is no way to determine that longevity in advance.

The ability to develop a mentoring relationship starts with the love of people. Have you ever met someone and shaken their hand and realized, I am never going to like this person or even associate with this person? To me, that is instinct, and 99% of the time your instincts are correct. I met a man years ago, and shaking his hand was the most uncomfortable thing I have ever done. I knew from the start I did not like him, even though he eventually became my boss, at which point my hatred for him became even worse. When he became my boss, the first thing he did was move me out of the office, saying, "I am the boss, and I deserve the bigger office." Kind of shows you what a small man he really was. I would have a difficult time doing that to an employee lower in position, and I would probably not do it. I just don't think it is proper to exert your power over another like that. Had this man waited, I may have given the office to him—well, probably not, considering the ass he truly was. Instincts (I can't explain them, but I sure as hell can feel them) have proven correct for me time and time again. Now, I will grant you that sometimes we make things come out the way we want simply from our actions, be it positive or negative, but a discussion around instincts is probably a topic for another book.

When I think back on people that influenced me most when I was growing up, I can come up with specific attributes my mentors taught me. If I were to be honest with myself (why not?), I could tell you where some of these habits and the way I approach situations came from. Whether it was teaching me how to act or how not to act, or exactly how to handle a situational problem, I have a variety of examples both ways, just as I am sure you do

Now this is me in May of 1959, striking my first deal on the phone. Influencing and the "gift of gab" started early.

Now, you know what really surprises me are the people who cannot go back to childhood and describe situations that either influenced them positively or negatively. I had tremendously strong grandmothers on both sides of my family. Both are now gone from this earth, but both were wise, caring, and compassionate. Now these were not Ivy League educated women, but they both weathered the great depression and came out of it stronger. Both had rough lives, but through all their trials and tribulations, they were still very kind and loving. They were the kind of influencers who were always there for you. Their doors were always open, whether you had a problem or you just wanted to stop and shoot the breeze. These were women of exceptional character, even though they had no status in life other than mother, wife, and grandmother.

As you will see in my stories that follow, influencers and mentors need not be great statesmen, politicians, or famous people. They are people who take an interest in you and love you, irrespective of your flaws and faults. They provide encouragement through the rough times and praise through the good times. Mentors come from all areas of life. You just need to recognize their being and acknowledge their existence and *use* their advice. My grandmothers taught me wisdom, how to really care for another, and how to have compassion for others. What a fantastic gift they left me with.

I had an uncle who was a butcher. Butchers, at that time, were big, gruff guys who tackled big sides of beef in a freezer or refrigerator most of the day. I didn't see this uncle much, because he lived an hour away, but I saw him a few times per year. When Uncle Herm used to drive us around, he used to ask, "Ronnie, what kind of car is that?" and I would answer him. When I didn't know what kind of car it was, he'd tell me. He got a big kick out of me answering him when he asked the question. What did that lead to? Well, maybe it led to my ability to carry on a conversation? Maybe it led to my ability to recognize and remember? I don't quite know, but obviously Uncle Herm was a big influence on my young life. Maybe that is why in the picture below, I am out selling cars in front of my parents' house at three or four years old.

That is all I can tell you over fifty years later. I wonder if I ever sold one.

I was blessed with another relationship with my Uncle Jack. A World War II veteran, Jack was the most selfless person I had ever met. Now, even though I admire him greatly and have tried to pattern myself after him, I could never hold a candle to Uncle Jack. You see, he was always giving his time to help others. I owned a duplex while newly married and Jack was an electrician by trade and a mighty good one. He worked in the mill, but when I called him with an electrical issue, he'd jump in his car and be there in a flash to fix the problem. When neighbors were in the hospital, Jack would go out and buy food for the family that remained home. When they were laid up or widowed, Jack would go cut their grass. He volunteered endlessly for the church and the Knights of Columbus, standing on the street corner in the rain, collecting money for the Special Olympics. You see, Jack was truly selfless, and all the while growing up, I had this angel on earth to teach me selflessness. Years later, at his funeral, my other uncle came up to me and said "Ron, we lost a good man." I turned to my uncle and said, "No, the world lost a great man".

You see, the true measure of a man is not what he thinks of himself, but what others think of him. I've always believed that, and I always will. That has been proven true to me a few times in my life. While traveling with my wife and daughter in Switzerland, a good friend took my daughter aside and told her there were a few things he wanted to tell her about her dad. I just walked away. The next day we flew up to Amsterdam and had dinner with another friend and his life. During dinner, he said, "Carly, there are a few things I want to tell you about your dad—this is what he taught me." I just excused myself to go to the restroom. My wife told me once, "Most people have good things said about them when they die; you have good things said about you while you live." That I learned from my Uncle Jack.

When you talked to Uncle Jack, the discussion was always about you, not him. Years later, when we had kids, the first thing out of Jack's mouth when he saw us, was to ask about the kids. He was a part of the greatest generation, certainly. I suppose there were many Jacks in that generation, and everyone probably has a story about their Uncle Jack. As Jack was on his death bed, dying from lung cancer, I knew he would love to see my daughter once again. So I brought her over, and his face lit up once again. You see, even in death, it was about Jack's selfless attitude and his way that made you comfortable. Because he cared more for you than himself, you realized just how important you were and how much you were empowered to do. I miss Uncle Jack, and there is not a day that goes by that I don't think of him and ask him to guide me selflessly. I know he is listening, and boy, do I miss him.

Another mentor of mine was my high school teacher, Bill. Bill was married to another teacher and every day I would see him and his wife walking to school together as I wrapped up the deliveries for my paper route. So I became familiar with him and his wife just by them passing me every day. I had Bill in ninth grade for home room and later in tenth and eleventh grade for history. What a great man. He was so personable and caring. He taught me compassion for others. He taught me patience, listening for the right answer, and how to rephrase the questions different ways so people understood. This came in handy when I started to do a lot of international business as many a colleague had complimented me on the way I could rephrase the statement or question to develop some sort of understanding. While teaching his class, he would look you right in the eye and ask a question. He had such an engaging way about him that I try to emulate him when doing live presentations. He taught me how to be genuine in an engagement with people and not just act like you care, but really care. Years later, people would ask me how I became so engaging in a discussion. I had a boss who once told me I was the most engaging person he had ever met. That's a pretty good compliment, I would say.

Bill was the guy who taught me how to connect, teach, listen, and make meaningful and thoughtful suggestions and recommendations. I suppose others who are maybe not as perceptive as me or certainly not as impressionable at the time, who had Bill as a teacher, might think nothing of him, but I learned a lot from that man. He taught me how to teach because he was a great teacher. But more importantly, he was a great, caring man. But those are behaviors that are learned, emulated, copied and repeated. We are influenced so much by others as we grow up and develop. That is the way to leave an everlasting impression on this world we take so much from.

I never had the kind of influencer or mentor in the business world that I have become to others. I don't know if my eyes weren't fully open to looking for that specific mentor or I just didn't recognize it for whatever other reason. I got caught up in the ugly political part of organizations, and that is probably why I have modified or changes careers over the past ten years. I was driving the other day with a friend in the car, and he was talking about his career and influencers. I obviously had keen interest in listening to him, with the ulterior motive of gathering more information for this book. He told me of his mentors and influencers, and how he stays in touch with these folks to this day. He talked of how certain people went out of their way to make him successful and plowed the way for his success. I think that his experience is a rare occurrence, and I think he is a lucky man to have people in the corporate world influence and mentor him. I don't necessarily know why I found none of that early on in life, but irrespective of that, I have chosen to give to others in such a way that I have been rewarded by mentoring in ways most can't even imagine. Maybe it's helped me to develop a deeper understanding of how and when mentoring is effective.

So, I am puzzled when I ask people who were the greatest influences in their lives and they are stymied and can't answer—because I can name Bill and Herm and Jack and so many more people who took the time and invested in me to show other ways of accomplishing goals, not just the traditional ways. Who are your mentors? Who has influenced you, and in what ways? I think it is very important to realize who those influencers are, both positive and negative, because when we find out our influences, we can find out our goals that much more clearly. It reminds me of the Seinfeld episode where Jerry brings up the subject of "Festivus" with George. George's dad walks into the scene and proclaims, "George, Festivus is your heritage." It is true—our past is our heritage, like it or not. Sometimes (hopefully) our influencers have been positive influencers on the people we have become, and if we are open enough and perceptive enough, we have taken what we have understood as good stuff from our mentors and formed our own unique personalities.

So take time to think about your influencers and just how they affected who you have become and if it has been a positive influence, tell your influencers. Make their day; show them what they have done to help you. A while back I happened to run into an old college professor I had when doing my undergraduate studies and I told him what an impact he had on my life. I told him how he got me to look at things differently and how he still influences what I do today. He looked surprised. It is not that often that someone tells us we made a difference in their lives, but it is a great feeling when they do. I have often said that 10% of the folks we have touched will tell us that we have touched them, but we have touched so many others who have not told us. You will not regret doing that. If you wait, time may pass you by and you will regret never having that conversation. It is a powerful conversation to have.

In his article "The Role of Mentoring," Mark Bloomberg reminds us of something Eleanor Roosevelt said: "Learn from the mistakes of others. You can't live long enough to make them all yourself," (88). A wise and experienced mentor helps us avoid mistakes, and Eleanor Roosevelt was a wise woman, certainly. A mentor can advise you on what to do and how to do it, but she can't do it for you. A good mentor will explain the plusses and minuses of the decision points and recommend a path, but also not be disappointed when his protégé takes another direction or puts his or hers own spin on the mentor's advice. You see, mentoring is built on the relationship and the act of the protégé learning, because mentoring is always development driven. Keep in mind (because someone always asks, "What is in it for me?") that there is nothing but fulfillment and satisfaction in it for the mentor. That is what drives the concept of mentoring.

Bloomberg also goes on to point out that everyone needs mentoring:

> Although we may not all be lucky enough to find someone who can fulfill that role, it is very clear from my own career that a mentor can only enhance one's skills and decision-making capabilities. It is simply easier and more satisfying to rely on the hard-earned experience of your mentor to enable you to avoid common pitfalls and embrace proven techniques. (88-89)

So true mentors are engaging conversationalists who care about you selflessly?

Mentors are genuinely concerned about their protégés. They provide their guidance and counsel out of a generosity of spirit. The mentor's performance is never tied to the protégé's, so it brings a certain objectivity that does not really exist in coaching. In mentoring, it is believed that the business input and personal input affect one another. Mentoring, in many cases, has a certain spiritual component that coaching does not have. Now, by spirit I am not referring to religion, but I'm focused more holistically on the well-being of the protégé.

"Mentoring is an exchange and you can leverage the relationship to benefit your own career," says Ellen Ensher, a management professor at Loyola Marymount University and co-author of *Power Mentoring.* In fact, research has found a link between becoming a sponsor and getting ahead; among graduates of twenty-six top business schools, those with protégés earned $25,075 more on average from 2008 to 2010 than colleagues who did no mentoring, workplace researcher Catalyst found.

Further, Donna Rosato, in her article "Benefit from Being a Mentor," referred to a study of Sun Microsystems employees by Capital Analytics and found that mentors were 20% more likely to get raises and six times more likely to receive promotions (44).

Paul Lawrence and Ann Whyte, in "Designing Leadership Development Programs—the Case for Coaching," point out that 62% of participants said their mentors were valuable, helping them understand the organization, providing advice based on their own experience and introducing participants to other people in the organization. Of those who said mentoring wasn't useful, many talked about how difficult it was to gain access to their mentor. For others, mentoring did not appear to meet their immediate needs, and some talked about the need to train mentors, with some mentors displaying greater skills than others in terms of being able to manage an effective mentoring conversation (11).

So, every day, it seems I have something more to add to this journal on mentoring, another example of how people just don't get what I am talking about, but wait...maybe they do. I was having lunch today with a young man who was in my marketing class when I taught undergrads. This guy is very bright, but with a hint of ADD, which hurts him in a sense. I asked him, "So what will you do after you finish your Master's?" He said, "I have been giving that some thought lately." I said, "You have to act now." I told him that I had invited him a number of times to meet some of my friends and connect with them. They can share their career goals and objectives so he develops a network of people to depend on and get input from, people that are closer to his age. I said, "Do you realize what an opportunity you are passing up here?" He said, "It took me a while, but now I realize what you are trying to do for me, and what a fool I am for passing it up. It took reading your book and listening to your podcasts to realize just what you are doing and how you are opening up other pathways for me. I did not fully realize that until I knew more about you." This builds the case for trust. Until you can prove the trust in a relationship, nothing else works. I am the lucky one, because I can take these little snippets of information and use them to mentor or coach people a little differently each time. You see, the educator or the mentor learns continuously too. There is a lot of power in being a mentor, so use that power wisely.

Takeaways

- Being a mentor requires being selfless.

- First, mentors must *lead* by guiding interaction with their protégés. Secondly, Mentors must *support* protégés.

- The ability to develop a mentoring relationship starts with the love of people.

- The true measure of a man is not what he thinks of himself, but what others think of him.

- It is very important to realize who our influencers are, both positive and negative, because when we find out our influences, we can find out our goals that much more clearly.

- Mentoring is built on the relationship and the act of the protégé learning, because mentoring is always development driven.

- Make a list of people who have been influential in helping you become who you are today. Describe what they actually did for you and how it affected you. Do you remember them being selfless, and if so, how so?

- Describe your strongest positive traits and examine where those abilities came from. Who were your greatest influencers? If you could thank them, what would you tell them?

Chapter Three:

What is a Coach?

When giving my presentation on mentoring and coaching, I always show Jim Caldwell on the coaching slide. Who is Jim Caldwell, you might ask? He is the current coach of the Detroit Lions. He has been a successful football coach with a number of teams, and he knows what it takes to win. He has also been through an awful season, in which he lost his star quarterback, so he knows how to lose as well. I am sure if you asked Mr. Caldwell which side he would rather be on, he would say the winning side. Although there are many great examples of successful coaches in the National Football League, I dwell on Jim for a couple of reasons. One, I am a Lions fan, and it is good to see such a solid coach and example as Mr. Caldwell lead my favorite team, but more importantly, it is the calmness and confidence he portrays while coaching a game. It is having the players' backs when they deserve his support and his discipline when they don't. You see, a coach leads a team. He or she does what is in the best interests of the team. The quickest, most athletic players play because they are going to score the most points or give up the fewest turnovers in a football game. It is about the game, not about the individual.

Where mentoring is about the individual, coaching is about the team. Coaches are known for motivating individuals within a team to perform. They are noted for their inspirational pep talks, for their inspiring plays, and for making the right moves at the right times. Not all coaches are good. Again, it takes years to develop the inspiration and wisdom to lead and to coach others. Just think of your local high school football coach and what he might have taught you, or how he might have inspired you to go the extra mile or reach back for something extra on the field. That is what good coaches do; they inspire you to contribute to the team's greatness. But make no mistake, it is about the team. The guy who would be better suited for the offensive line is not going to get to run the ball as the halfback. You see, there is no "I" in team; it is about the team. The smooth-fielding shortstop who can't hit a lick, he may be just as valuable as the star pitcher or the first baseman who hits thirty home runs, because he fills a void on the team. This is also what good business coaches do, they inspire the team to hit their goals and exceed delivery performance.

Business coaches are focused on specific behaviors to improve and enhance, which is one reason why coaching has exploded within the business community. Coaching is proven way to increase the effectiveness of employees in the workplace. In fact, Damian Goldvarg, in "The Building Blocks of Great Coaching," says, "...an Executive Coaching study by Gerald Olivero, K. Denise Bane, and Richard E. Kopelman showed that a program combining training and coaching increased participants' productivity by 88 percent, versus the 22.4 percent increase shown by managers enrolled in a training-only program," (54).

Another reason that coaching has exploded in popularity in recent years is because many existing workplace training programs are not as effective as they could be, and adding a coaching component is a great way to supplement these programs. Eman Taie, in "Coaching as an

Approach to Enhance Performance," tells us that, "Education and training alone are not enough to produce the results that organizations need to remain competitive. For this reason, coaching is an educational technique that bridges the gap between learning and practice or between training and the workplace," (34). Insightful managers and employers need to learn how to correctly implement a coaching program in their organizations, because coaching is a valuable, and increasingly necessary, tool in today's dog-eat-dog workplace. A successful and well run coaching program can not only make employees more skilled in their jobs and maximize their morale, but it also has the capacity to increase their loyalty, since through these programs employees will come to understand that their employers are invested in their success.

You don't have to take my word for it. Several experts agree that the ability to keep talented employees is one of the main keys to running a successful company. Dan Steer is one of these experts. In "Onboard with it All," he writes, "If you want to save on future recruitment costs and keep knowledge in-house, retention is a key matter to address," (27). And According to Stephen Morel, in "Onboarding Secures Talent for the Long Run," "New employees decide whether or not to stay at a company within their first six months of employment. Those who are engaged on the first day of work, according to the Aberdeen Group's Onboarding Benchmark Report, have a greater incentive to stay."

Now, you might be saying, "Easier said than done," and I agree. It's easy to talk about keeping employees, but how do we actually do that? Through mentoring and coaching. Kerry Little, citing Ziggi Leijens, writes, "Lejins sees how mentoring contributes to Treasury's ability to attract and attain the best graduates, best thinkers and most motivated young people..." (29). Mentoring and coaching programs are the easiest way to show employees that you are serious about them and dedicated to their success. These programs are the best way to build trust and facilitate communication, which in turn builds a healthy organization.

This does not mean that coaching programs are a one-stop solution for every problem your business might be facing. Betsy Morris, in "So You're a Player. Do You Need a Coach?" brings up a valid point when she writes, "At many companies, coaching has become the Band-Aid for a lot of the dysfunction caused by the trial and error of doing business in new ways." Band-Aids can't cure diseases. Coaching programs, especially improperly implemented ones, are not the be-all and end-all of a company's success. Sometimes coaching is not the solution—sometimes mentoring is what's called for. It's important to know when people need to be coached and when they need to be mentored, and to do that, we need to know the differences between these two ideas.

To understand the difference between a coach and a mentor, we will start to fill in The Mentor Matrix we find later in this book. This will help identify exactly what a mentor does and what a coach does and how they are different in each instance. You will also be able to see how each of those concepts are different from a standard business relationship. Why is this important to know? Because you will be able to determine which actions you need to take to support the relationship you are trying to achieve. Each action is going to require you to spend a small amount of effort or a large amount as well as devotion or dedication. It will all center on the end result you are trying to achieve as well.

Defined by the International Coach Federation (ICF) as "partnering with clients in a thought-provoking and creative process that inspires them to maximize their personal and professional potential," coaching is used to help individuals dramatically improve their outlook on work and life, while honing their leadership skills and unlocking their potential. The ICF sees coaching as establishing building blocks for personal growth, and I can certainly see that, because coaching is far more structured than mentoring—having specific goals and deliverables in mind. Remember, coaching is shorter term than mentoring, and it is performance driven. The person being coached does not typically need to be trained on understanding the coaching relationship. Coaches are outside knowledge experts that stay with you for a defined period of time and usually leave when the coaching is finished. The process of being coached allows the employee or the person being coached to perform better—be it on a sports team or in a business relationship.

Another way to look at the spread of coaching is that it bridges the growing chasm between what managers are being asked to do and what they have been trained to do. It is almost like the difference between generals in peacetime and generals in war, says Betsy Morris, quoting Harvard's John Kotter, writes, "We have a lot of people who were trained to be superb managers but now have horrendous leadership challenges thrown at them. I think a lot of the coaching is aimed at trying to help people develop skills and actions that are different from what they grew up with," (144-54).

Taie reminds us of the ICF's definition of coaching, then goes on to give us other aspects of that definition: "Coaching is defined as the art and practice of inspiring, energizing, and facilitating the performance, learning, and development of the coachee," (34). Coaching is used to help individuals dramatically improve their outlook on work and life, while also honing their leadership skills and unlocking their potential. Taie also tells us that, "Most coaches would agree that coaching is a unique and individually-tailored intervention that enables individuals to explore and address real life challenges and to develop his/her vision and sense of purpose," (34). Success and fulfillment in life and in business are often linked, and a coaching program, properly implemented, will do much more than make for a short-term gain—it will provide an employee with the foundations for bringing that short-term accomplishment into the future.

Clinton Longenecker, in "Coaching for better results: key practices of high performance leaders," tells us that while the word "coach" can mean many different things to many people, our research strongly suggests that a coach is an individual who is in a position to provide feedback, counsel and accountability to another individual with the purpose of helping them improve their performance and develop their talents, (33). In my book, however, I claim that the difference between a coach and a mentor is the output. In a mentoring relationship, the output is the individual. In a coaching relationship, the output is the team or something larger than the individual.

That is why, I would argue, there is a huge difference between being coached and being mentored. Not only is the time frame much different, the purpose is much different as well. Coaching concerns itself with performance right now, while the nature of mentoring becomes much more established over the course of the relationship. Consequently, coaching is a more limited relationship, but sometimes a limited approach, with short term goals, is what's called for. Mentoring takes a lot of time to implement effectively, and sometimes businesses just don't have the luxury of time. The key here is to know the situation and use the best option for your situation. Most organizations today use the term coaching because they are trying to enhance performance and get people focused on the short term. That is what makes it very different from a mentoring relationship, because most of those relationships have an extended period of time in which they are deployed.

- Insightful managers and employers need to learn how to correctly implement a coaching program in their organizations, because coaching is a valuable, and increasingly necessary, tool in today's dog-eat-dog workplace.

- The ability to retain talented employees is one of the main keys to running a successful company. We retain talented employees through mentoring and coaching programs.

- Coaching is far more structured than mentoring—having specific goals and deliverables in mind. Remember, coaching is shorter term than mentoring, and it is performance driven.

- In a mentoring relationship, the output is the individual. In a coaching relationship, the output is the team or something larger than the individual.

Exercises

- Who are the best coaches you have seen? What do they all have in common? How do they motivate the people they are engaged with, and what types of rewards do they use?

- From the good coaches you have seen, just how do their skills differ from any mentoring relationship you may have had?

Chapter Four:

Differences between Mentors and Coaches

We've already talked about a few of the differences between mentoring and coaching. Mentoring focuses on long term investment in a relationship between a mentor and a protégé. Coaching focuses on the short term; it isn't as relationship oriented, and it looks more to the success of a group.

Many times coaches are judged based on noticeable, immediate results, and if the results are not as noticeable or as immediate as bosses are looking for, then, well, that coach is moving on to the next team. Mentors are not judged based on immediate results, and sometimes the effect of their work won't even be noticed until months or years into the relationship. The mentoring process is much more holistic in nature, focusing on the complete well-being of both parties, as opposed to one specific project.

Think about it this way: it's a matter of having the best tool for the job. Say, for instance, that you have a brand new chainsaw—a Husqvarna or an Echo, or whatever kind you've had your eye on.

Would you use that chainsaw to hammer in a nail? No. That would be ridiculous. A chainsaw has its job and a hammer has its job, and comparisons can't even be made without bringing a smile to your face. While the differences between mentoring and coaching are much subtler, they still exist, and sometimes one is the right choice when the other just won't work for the task at hand.

Wayne Hart, in "What is Mentoring?" puts it this way:

> While coaching typically focuses on enhancing current job performance, mentoring focuses on career path. Mentors typically use coaching skills a great deal as they endeavor to guide a mentee; in this regard they manage the relationship, guide and counsel, motivate and inspire, serve as models, and rely heavily on questioning and listening skills. (P 7-8)

There you have it; a completely different skill set is involved for each one. A coach needs to be able to motivate; he has to be able to inspire. A mentor needs to know how to listen and really understand his protégé's issues. But the two areas do overlap, and this is the important point. Sometimes a coach needs to listen in order to motivate, and sometimes, after listening, a mentor needs to be able to motivate his or her protégé.

In addition to skill sets, mentoring and coaching are also distinguished by the personalities involved. Speaking of this, Philip Perry, in "Smart Mentoring: When Skilled Employees Share Their Knowledge," says, "While the process is similar to coaching, mentoring usually targets more subtle skills requisite to the enhancement of career potential," (P. 46). Mentoring may not be as flashy as coaching, and a mentor might go unnoticed and un-thanked for years, but at the end of the process, those who mentor may find that it is just as rewarding, if not much more, than coaching others.

Benefits of Mentoring and Coaching

Now that we've talked about the differences between the two areas, let's talk about the benefits involved in both. There are so many benefits to a coaching and mentoring relationship, and these are seldom one sided. Years ago, I had a young man who worked for me in Toronto. Now, Duncan was a very bright young engineer, recently graduated from college, working for me as a commodity manager in a very large electronics company. He was probably one of the brightest individuals I have ever met. One day, while working on his Performance Development Plan, I gave him a little sticky note with four or five adjectives on it that described the things that might hold him back from fully developing his career. These were words such as "stubborn," "idealistic," and a few others I can't quite recall now. I handed Duncan the sticky note and told him we would do his review the next day, and to think about the five adjectives and how they applied to him before the review. The next day, Duncan came in and told me he had talked to his father that night about the adjectives that I used to describe him, and I asked him, “Well what did your father have to say about that?” He told me his father asked, “How does Ron know you so well in such a short period of time?” We had a successful meeting on the PDP and I told him these things, if not addressed, would limit him from a career development perspective. He understood where I was going with this. I did this strictly to help him, with no agenda of my own.

Years later, while travelling in Europe, I called Duncan and asked him to meet me in Zurich for dinner. He did, and when he came, he walked up in his Hugo Boss suit, put his portfolio down on the table, and opened it up…there was the sticky note I had written five years prior. I was stunned to see it, and he told me, “There is not a day that goes by that I don’t look at that and figure out how to address those issues.” What a great time for the mentor as well as the protégé. Those are the times you realize you have made enough of an impression on someone that they have taken your advice to heart. He is successful now, and I have to credit his drive and ambition for persevering, but maybe I had a hand in helping him mold himself into that success. Maybe just a little…

Since we are on the subject of knowing when you have had an effect on someone by what you have done, I will tell you another little story. I had an employee, who was to do his Performance Development Plan (A PDP was a plan of action for all employees to plan out the year, capture what they learned the past year and rate their performance), but he told me he hadn't learned a thing from his previous boss (he had just started working for me in Q4), so he didn't feel it was necessary to do his PDP. When he told me this, I said that he was a big boy and he could decide whether he wanted to do one or not. His rationale was that, since he hadn't learned anything from his old boss, he had nothing to write. Come the end of the year it was bonus time and my boss came up to me and asked why this young man had not completed his PDP. Since his old boss did not get one from him, he ranked him a three (which meant he was eligible for no bonus that year. The proper response from the ex-boss (no

PDP=no bonus). I explained the situation to him and said he should rate the employee a two, so he would get his normal bonus, and I would take care of the situation. I carefully thought, "How am I going to make this a learning experience for this employee?" I sat the employee down and told him just what effect his decision had on his bonus, but not to worry, "I pulled your ass out of the fire, and you will be getting your bonus, but you will be writing your PDP, and here is how to do it." I have always found it is best to diffuse a bad situation and try to turn it into a learning event for the protégé. This was an opportunity for the protégé to learn as well as for the mentor to create deeper bonds because of the fact I had solved the problem already.

So I took him step by step through how to look at new learning experiences, how to analyze just what he had learned and why he had learned it—a lot of inter-reflective stuff about his personality and how he learned and absorbed. Every few days he would bring in a revision to the PDP, and we would sit down and go over what he had learned.

It turns out, he had learned quite a bit that year. I know he surprised himself. By the time we had made the twentieth revision and he was close to being final with it at fourteen pages, he came to me and proudly handed the document over. I said, "What are you giving this to me for?" He said, "I completed all this work....and you aren't even going to read it?" I said, "I could have written it for you, but you had to do it. The only way for you to learn is to reflect and determine just what you got out of your work this year. You wrote this for you, not me." This was another lesson for the protégé. It's now years later, and in both of these cases the relationship continues, the dialogue continues, and so does the advice, but rather than advice *per se,* it is just another input, just another perspective, just another opinion for the protégé to absorb and spit out as his or her decision.

I think when you find that you put yourself in someone else's shoes, you will see things differently. That is why mentoring and being mentored is so cool, because the learning never stops. I am proud to say I have mentored and

Be reflective and observant of others behaviors and actions

have been mentored. It has taught me to be reflective and observant of others' behaviors and actions.

I also believe that no matter who we are or what stage of life we are in, the value of a mentor or a coach is immeasurable. In most cases a mentor or coach can help you avoid the pitfalls of business or your personal life. They can, through their experiences, help you to navigate uncharted waters in your career or your personal life. I liken it to getting an MBA. If you do not go to a top ten school, the other thousand programs are about the same. If you have a mentor who is willing to share life experiences with you, it can add another dimension to your education, just like the MBA does or would. When I look back on my career and its many successes—as well as failures—I think about the times I did not have a mentor to guide me through some of the failures, and based on what I know today, just how easily those could have been turned into successes. If I might have had someone to bounce ideas off of, we may have been in better shape to turn those things around, and they wouldn't have been so destructive.

- A completely different skill set is involved for mentoring and coaching, but the two areas do sometimes overlap. Sometimes a coach needs to listen in order to motivate, and sometimes, after listening, a mentor needs to be able to motivate his or her protégé.

- Mentoring teaches us to be reflective and to be observant of others' behaviors and actions.

- Mentors help individuals achieve their personal and professional goals, while coaches affect their teams' results.

Exercises

- Contrast the differences in your experiences as a protégé and a coachee. What have the differences been? Which relationships have lasted the longest? Which have given you more fulfillment?

- Think about a time when someone gave you advice that ran contrary to your thinking on a particular subject. What did you do? Did you take the advice? Did you decide not to take it? Why or why not? Either way, what was your decision based on? Did trust play a role in it?

Chapter Five:

I am a Farmer, and maybe You Should be, Too

I've told this story many times, and still get laughs out of it every time I do. One time, as I was having lunch with a relatively new associate, he asked what I did for a living. I told him I was a farmer. Now after he spit his food out and laughed insatiably for a few minutes, I explained to him what I meant. You see I have always thought of myself as blessed, actually in many different ways…first of all, I have seen almost the entire world on someone else's dime (business), and this has allowed me to gain a perspective on the world most others can't quite see or even grasp. I was diagnosed with a couple of auto-immune deficiency diseases early in life, so, I catch a lot of colds and don't necessarily have the ability to fight the bugs off. Because of this, I believe in one thing most importantly—I am on earth to touch people and make a difference in their lives. These unfortunate circumstances are really fortunate, because they give me a different perspective on life and living. I have often sat down and asked myself why I continue to live while others with the same affliction die. The only rational explanation I can come up with is that the Lord must be looking to get more out of me. So I try to figure out what that means on a daily basis. How can I contribute and make a lasting contribution?

But what does that have to do with farming, you may ask?

Webster says a farmer is one who cultivates land or crops or raises animals. What is a person who raises or cultivates people? I can't tell you the amount of times I have reached out to a complete stranger and struck up a conversation, whether it is on a plane, train, or just blindly on social media. I like to see the shock on peoples' faces when I do such things. It is comical sometimes. Now sometimes the recipient of my advances is shocked by my forwardness, but in most cases, they reach back out. Why, you have to ask yourself? Are they searching for the elusive golden ring of knowledge, are they looking for friendship, or are they simply looking for some little snippet of knowledge they feel they are lacking to make their lives more complete or fulfilled? I don't know, I guess that depends on the recipient. A farmer does the same thing. A farmer plants seeds and provide sustenance for his family and many other families. A farmer also fertilizes, cultivates, and comes back to reap the harvest. I believe in patterning myself as a farmer. When it comes to relationships, I believe you first plant a seed and make the relationship fertile enough to grow. You come back to cultivate that growth, and when the time is right, the plant benefits, as well as the farmer. When there is benefit for both parties, it is time for harvest. Harvest time is success for everyone. It benefits all parties because bellies get filled, and both parties can enjoy the fruits of their labor. Both have reached a state of fulfillment, in a sense.

When it comes to building relationships, farming is the perfect activity. Relationships grow that way. When you have cultivated the seeds and come back to water the plant, and the plant produces, there is satisfaction for the farmer. The same is true in building relationships, when you have started the conversation and figured out how to make both parties satisfied. Now, because you really understand all of the needs, you can fill the role of the farmer. The farmer's goal is to produce the largest, best-tasting, healthiest fruit or vegetable possible. It is just like entering the county fair as proud as can be, because of the farmer's labor. It's the same with the relationship farmer as well.

Now the first question would be, exactly how do you do this? I say you always make it about the other person, never about you. Find a common platform on which to engage. Find some common theme to start the conversation. It can be family, cars, careers, whatever—it just has to be a common interest between the two of you. Many times when you hit that common thread people will really open up—in fact, sometimes you find out more than you really wanted to know, so be careful and listen.

I remember years ago, a business associate I had recently met told me his wife worked for United Airlines. I filed that fact in the back of my mind (I always try to remember something about everyone), and about seven or eight years later I ran into Larry and asked him if his wife still worked for United or if she had retired. He asked me, how did you know my wife worked for United? I told him, "Because you told me so many years ago." He walked away, either astonished at my memory or astonished that I had miraculously recreated this bond between him and I after all these years.

Remembering key details is an easy way of reestablishing relationships, and I have made a habit of trying to remember something about everyone. This especially works well with friends from other countries, as most people do not consider Americans too sincere. I have always tried to immerse myself in another culture whenever I am in a foreign land.

Indians are a unique group. I have great friendships with my Indian friends because I have never refused to go to temple with them; I have always tried to understand their culture. One time, while I was in Delhi for a plant opening, we had a ceremony to bless the new manufacturing equipment that had been recently installed in our plant, and they had a priest come into do the blessing. They tied little red strings around my wrists, and I kept mine on until they fell off. A few months later, my friend from India was visiting and he asked me why I kept the bracelet on? I told him that it reminded me of my friends in India. He was speechless. And that is exactly why I kept it on, even though my boss cut his off on the plane home. You see, I think it is an honor to take some small bit of another's culture and immerse it with ours, as it broadens the respect we have for one another. It certainly does make the world a smaller place. Now, isn't that farming?

Strange as it may sound, I cannot tell you how many conversations with people I have met on airplanes that have turned into longer term relationships. Now, I understand that sometimes we are just exhausted from our trips, business, and our everyday lives, and we are in no mood to open up to strangers, but it is really funny how sometimes these relationships start. One day, while traveling to Western Canada, I struck up a conversation with a gentleman who looked to be about my age. He was reading *Car and Driver,* so the conversation started with vehicles. This is a pretty common way to start a conversation with another man. That conversation turned into architecture and art and music, and it pretty much covered the three hour flight. Long story short, we had more in common than you might have imagined. He was also a consultant, and we stay in touch to this day. It is a small world, and we don't realize it's getting smaller all the time. I have dozens of stories like this, but I think you get the point.

Farmers are the salt of the earth, and such an integral part to our viability and success. Farmers understand conservation and the thought behind replenishing assets. If the land is not taken care of for future generations, there will be no future. So a farmer is one to be admired and someone we need to look up to because of his stature and character; he is always doing what is right for the future. We have to take a lesson from farmers as we farm in the field of relationships. We need to always be looking to the future, looking to the bigger picture. We need to look for opportunities as they show themselves, and not just be limited to the present moment. Because, as we say, if we don't, we will have no future.

Let's also take a lesson from farmers when it comes to harvesting. In our farming analogy, we have planting, and we have growing, and we finally come to harvesting. Harvesting is when we profit from the relationship. Remember, the goal of mentor/protégé relationships is the "win-win" paradigm, and to get there, both parties must benefit. The protégé benefits from the mentor's experience, and the mentor benefits from the excitement and raw potential of the protégé. When we as mentors get to see our protégés blossom and become the dynamic people we knew they could be, we get a sense of satisfaction that can't be beat. There's nothing like knowing you have had an impact on someone else's life.

Now, don't you want to be a farmer?

I am proud to call myself a farmer, although not in the sense you might expect.

- When it comes to relationships, first plant a seed and make the relationship fertile enough to grow; then come back to cultivate that growth; then, when there is benefit for both parties, it is time for harvest.

- In order to begin the process of mentoring, always make it about the other person, never about you. Find a common platform on which to engage.

- Remembering key details is an easy way of reestablishing relationships.

- We need to always be looking to the future, looking to the bigger picture. We need to look for opportunities as they show themselves, and not just be limited to the present moment.

Exercises

- Think of times you have had to play the role of farmer and plant seeds. Make a short timeline of all the things that had to happen for that relationship to be successful and bear fruit. Describe the process.

- Think of a relationship that you would currently like to cultivate. How can you use the lessons in this chapter to build that relationship and make it robust?

Chapter Six:

Character and Integrity

If you are my friend or I am your friend, it is based on three things—trust, character, and integrity. Things don't always go as planned. Believe me, I know firsthand, but if we can depend on each other like family and we trust one another, it makes it so much easier. I think that philosophy is true whether you are my mentor, I am your mentor, you are my coach, I am your coach, or we just have a great business relationship.

None of us are flawless. We all make mistakes. Sometimes we do the wrong things, and each of us sometimes pays dearly when we do. I have always believed in honesty being the best policy, not because I am of such high moral standards, although I hope some might say that, but perhaps because of a little simpler explanation. I am a man, and if I lie, I can't necessarily remember who I lied to. You see, I have caught people in lies or stretching the truth, and I think it is rather embarrassing if you catch someone in it. I have made a habit not to lie. Again, remember, we all have flaws and we are imperfect—unfortunately, God has not made the perfect human yet, but the only things we have to sell someone else are our honesty, our character, and our integrity. That is what our reputations are built upon.

Geri Leder, in "An Anchor in Stormy Seas," asks us to "[t]hink of two people—one whom you admire and one whom you distrust. Determine how you would answer these three questions about them: Can I trust you? Are you committed to excellence? And do you care about me?" (100). If you can't answer these simple questions about an individual, I would say there is a serious character issue present. In many cases it isn't just a lukewarm feeling. I have mentioned my daughter in a number of examples in this book, and in many cases these examples always remind me of stories with her. We were in Brooklyn having dinner one night when she had just started her job as a recruiter for a large retailer. I told her to be the best recruiter she could be by doing things others wouldn't do. I told her to actually care about the people she was placing, and to follow up with them once she had landed them, so she could develop a trusting relationship with them. I told her, “It will serve you well in your career.”

A few years later she was promoted into a different role and had some workplace issues come up. She called me and asked me if she should use her company’s human resources department as a sounding board for some of the issues. My immediate answer was no, but I decided to ask her one simple question: “Can you trust them?” When she responded, “Not really,” I told her the choice was clear. Again, it comes down to a matter of trust. Do you trust the individual you are speaking to enough to get your point across effectively without any retribution? I have some positive instances I can give you as well as some negative ones, and they all depend on the trusting relationship I either had or didn’t have. Even when I thought I had the utmost respect from and had great relationships with people, I quickly learned that they might turn on me. So it is very difficult to confide in someone who can’t wait to go running to the boss to turn you in for some insane issue. Today I trust no one but my kids, family, and close personal friends, and certainly, from a business perspective, I am guarded with most. That is exactly why you need a mentor. You need someone you can confide in who is looking out for you alone, not the forty-some people they supervise, not the six thousand people in the organization they are responsible for—just you and you alone. That is why I love mentoring; it gets you out of the politics business…

Shirley Chan, in "People Management in the Context of Global Change," writes, "Trustworthiness in human relationships is bred when it is known that the individuals involved possess personal integrity and will choose honorable behavior if tempted to deviate from right principles," (23). In the case mentioned above, with the folks in human resources, I couldn't bank on that. They weren't trustworthy. But trustworthiness is the quality that attracts clients and generates referrals. As we test for that quality in our own dealings, we can ask similar questions of ourselves: Do I act in ways consistent with earning the trust of others? Have I been sufficiently committed to excellence? How do I demonstrate it to my peers, contacts and clients? Am I as courteous as I expect them to be? If not, what actions can I take to raise the bar? (Leder, 100). Isn't that is what it is about—raising the bar and committing to excellence? We talk continually about process improvement, so shouldn't we also be talking about how we can improve our mentoring and coaching standards as well?

Commitment is a key part of character. One of the lessons I have taught my children is that when you make a commitment, it is etched in stone. If you say I will help you move on Saturday, you had better be there Saturday, helping your friend to move. I believe your word is your bond. If you have no intent of showing up on Saturday, then say that, but if you commit, the only thing that prevents you from living up to your commitment is death—either yours or mine.

What is character? Webster defines it as, "The way someone thinks, feels, and behaves: someone's personality: a set of qualities that are shared by many people in a group, country, etc.: a set of qualities that make a place or thing different from other places or things." I think that the first thing people see when they look at you is your character. Now, it's not fully exposed until you become friends, but we all like to hang around with people who are like ourselves, and I hope we think of ourselves as having the utmost character.

Character is a pattern of behavior, thoughts and feelings based on universal principles, moral strength, and integrity—including the ability to live by those principles every day. Character is evidenced by your life's virtues and the "line you never cross, or the things you would never do; it is the set of guiding principles by which we live our lives." Character is the most valuable thing you have, and nobody can ever take it away. Like a good education, and just like your experience from "the school of hard knocks," character is yours and yours alone.

Why is character so important to us all?

Character is who we are. Character in life is what makes people believe in you and believe in what you can do for them. It is the basis of establishing relationships and is essential both for individual success and for our society to function successfully. Society is based on the cooperation of a collection of individuals and each individual must do his or her part every day by living a life full of integrity. Integrity is the quality of being honest and having strong moral principles; moral uprightness. The more we pay attention to our character and integrity the more successful we will beat developing and sustaining relationships.

Integrity is adhering to a moral code of honesty, courage, strength and truthfulness—being true to your word and true to yourself as well. When you don't exhibit integrity, other people get hurt. But you hurt yourself even more, because when you think about it, hurting someone else is really hurting you. When you cheat, your "success" is false, and it is not sustainable. When you break a promise, you are showing that your word is meaningless. When you lie, you deceive others and lose their respect. When you lose respect, the relationship sours and the mentoring, coaching, or business relationship starts to unravel and dissolve. All of those examples destroy your reputation and break the trust others have in you. Without your good reputation and trustworthiness, your relationships fail. And often we reflect and ask ourselves, "Why?" You need to be believable and of the utmost character, I have said this many times, and those of you who know me well will be saying, "Here we go again." I learned early in life to be honest, but not because I was striving for honesty—you see, my memory just isn't that good. So when I fabricate a story, I can never remember what story I fabricated and just who I might have told it to. So I quickly learned to tell the truth, figuring that that way I won't get caught in a lie and accidentally hurt my character rating with any of my associates. It is good to know yourself sometimes...

How do good relationships equate to success?

Relationships are the foundation for success in life. This is the key, no matter what level the relationship is....mentor, coach, business partner, spouse, or friend. Those with strong relationship values have a better chance of succeeding in life because they have created a bigger safety net. For example, when you destroy the relationships with your friends, you will have no friends. You will be isolated and alone. You will look for other things to occupy your time, and typically those things are no good. They could be food, cigarettes, gambling, drugs, or many other vices. We look to fill that void because we are untrusted by our friends. If a student promises not to cheat, but does anyway, he is taking unfair advantage to put himself ahead of others without deserving it. He can ruin his reputation, his academic record, and his job prospects forever. When a businessman makes a promise to customers and doesn't deliver, he destroys his relationships with his customers. His customers go elsewhere and his business fails. His reputation is always at stake. And remember, all we really have to sell is ourselves...our character.

By breaking your relationships, you break the foundation for success in your life. What is true success? In many cases, true success isn't measured by us. For example, who is more successful, someone who is famous and makes a great deal of money, or someone who has no fame and makes little money, but is a great parent? Today in school, too much emphasis is being placed on good grades and high test scores—so much so that these things, rather than good character, are how we are defining success. I have always said that the true measure of success is not measured by us, but by others. The more respect and trust someone gives you is one true measure of success. Ask your friends, or be open to your protégés' telling you what they think of your mentoring ability. Ask them where you might be able to improve, and get better at giving them exactly what they want. Think about the people who you consider to be successful. What do they have that you don't? They don't proclaim themselves successful. It is a title that you bestow on others, and how exactly is it measured? Do we measure it by the vehicles they drive, the clothes they wear? Most likely, we make a character judgment--don't we? That is why character is so important.

Your good character is the most important asset you have. It takes a lifetime to build, but it can be lost in an instant. Once lost, it is difficult to regain. Your true character is revealed when no one else is looking. Often, people decide to act based on short term gain, or an easy fix to a problem, and they end up doing the wrong thing. The old adage "you are what you do" is true. Failing to consider the long term consequences of your acts can be disastrous. By study and focusing on the importance of character, you will be guided to do the right thing by principles, moral strength, and integrity. Nothing is more important for true success in your life. Developing character is our lives journey, and we must work at it daily in order to successful. We will stumble and fall, but when we realize it is about our partners, not us, we will be successful.

So many times in my career I have run into folks who just don't understand how important a person's character is. That is really too bad, because in most of those cases, these individuals have not had a proper mentoring relationship in their lives. I know of one case where a father took his son in to run his business and the son, over a period of time, drove the business into bankruptcy through a series of unscrupulous activities, drug issues and other trust-centered issues. The son's marriage failed, too, because he was always seeking affirmation. He did not realize that what others think of you is more important, as compared to what you think of yourself. How sad to ruin a business (that had one hundred and fifty employees at one time) over your own ego and trust issues. It makes one wonder if all of this could have been prevented had the son had a good mentor to guide him in his life and business ventures. One will never know, but the destruction left behind is really sad…a life and a family ruined.

The late civil rights leader Martin Luther King Jr. encouraged his followers not to judge people by their appearance, but by the content of their character. A person's character, be it good or bad, can inspire others to greatness. In business, the role of leadership-caliber character can never be understated. Authentic leaders lead from a strong, personal, moral value that can have a profound effect on their organizations and have a tremendous effect on their ability to mentor others as well. You need to understand how character affects your organization, and how it can attract top performers, and just what overall effect on performance it has on the tangible side. Monica Patrick, in an article for *The Houston Chronicle* says:

> People with good character genuinely care about the people they work with. While a respectful distance must be maintained in working relationships, genuine concern for others is important for small business. Teams are often smaller than groups in large companies, commanding a greater need for stronger inner-company ties. This character attribute may manifest as caring concern, helpfulness, and compassion.

This is so true when we talk about a person's character, but what other attributes typically come up? Trust, compassion, and genuine care for the rest of your team are additional benefits received by having a mentoring program in place at your business, or as a matter of course of doing business.

A good friend of mine, Michael Ross, who wrote *"Overcoming the Character Deficit—How to Restore America's Greatness One Decision at a Time,"* said it best when he asked, "What happens when we lose sight of the impact of our choices?" Everything we do in our lives has consequences, and the earlier we understand that, the better off we are. How many times have we regretted what we said, or more importantly, what we did?

Michael says in his book "that the word character is a deviation of the Greek word *charakter* which literally means the "stamp of a coin." American coins feature great men like Washington, Jefferson, Lincoln and Roosevelt. Their characters helped shape and set a high standard for our nation. The penny says *honest, perseverant,* and *humble*. The nickel says *creative, diplomatic,* and *competent*. The dime says *resolve, relationships,* and *patience*. The quarter says *courage, fortitude, and honor."* I say, isn't this the way we all want to be described?

Isn't this the legacy with which we would all like to live? People today don't think of their characters as being honest and humble or creative, diplomatic and competent, or full of courage, honor, and fortitude. But what if they did? Would this world not be a much better place to live if they did? I am sure the Greatest Generation (described by Tom Brokaw in his writings) would all agree that those words are very important, but somewhat lost in 2015. If they are less important today, why is that, and how powerful might they be if we embraced them? Would we not have fine moral character?

I mention in my first book (*The Dysfunctional Organization*), the vacuum of leadership in the world today. I mentioned a story about a time I was driving through South Africa with a good friend, who is a South African of British descent, and we were talking of statesmen. The question came up, are there any great statesmen or women in the world today? Of course, being in South Africa, my friend mentioned Nelson Mandela. Now Mandela has a checkered past, especially if you talk to the white population of South Africa. But in my humble opinion, here is what is amazing about Mandela. When F.W. DeKlerk gave up power to Mandela's party, everyone expected the worst. Everyone expected that power in the hands of Mandela would mean the demise of the nation. Give Nelson Mandela some admiration for realizing he needed white South Africa to help transform black South Africa, and that they had to work together with the minority who had been in power for years—many times oppressively—to make South Africa a great nation. His personal greed or vindictiveness for spending the best years of his life in Robben Island Prison was seldom apparent. This wise gentleman realized that in order to set up a successful future, he had to deal with the past, he had to allow a reasonable transition and that it was better for South Africa if he did. See, statesmen do what is right for their country, not necessarily what is right for them, either socially or politically. In that case, Mandela was a true statesman.

Who might be the others over the past fifty to one hundred years? Maybe Bill Clinton, Ronald Reagan, Margaret Thatcher, Tony Blair? You can certainly throw in Roosevelt and Winston Churchill into that discussion. Much has been written over the past few years of Roosevelt's slyness and his moxie, and at the same time his valued relationship with Churchill. FDR knew it would be political suicide to support the UK early on in the war, but Churchill was a friend and a staunch ally. They had a pact that when Churchill needed help the most, FDR would pull the string, and that is exactly what happened—and the world was saved from a tyrannical leader, be it Hitler, Stalin or someone else. As they say, the rest is history.

Now, we are not great men or women like these folks, but what will be our legacy? How will we contribute to the world—in albeit a smaller way—but still making this world a better place to live? It is through our character. It is doing the right thing at the right time in the best interest of the most people. It is letting go of the natural tendencies to hold spite, be vindictive, and pay back someone who has done us wrong. It is character that defines who we are.

Michael Ross argues that there is a character deficit in our nation today, and I can't argue with that. How did we lose our way, and what do we do to fix it? He will tell you that there are serious flaws within our political structure, the way we do business today, our health, our finances, our educational structure, our religious organizations, arts and entertainment, as well as our basic family structure. Now I would find any number of people agreeing with him, but the fact of the matter remains, how do we fix what has already been damaged? Michael will tell us "that each of us is not as important as all of us," and that we need to take a stand "to bring character back into our lives," and I agree wholeheartedly with him. The character deficit and understanding of what makes something deficient helps us to remedy it today when you decide to take action and fix it. It is really all about the action we take when we look at character from a mature perspective. It shows us what we need to do to build a strong nations, strong families, and strong relationships, and be effective once again.

What does this have to do with mentoring, you might ask? And I am glad you did, because character is a key part of any relationship. Whether it is a mentoring/protégé relationship, a coaching relationship, a business relationship, or the relationship between spouses, character is such a key part.

> Outside the realm of people I have known personally, I have come to admire legendary football coach, Lou Holtz. Early on in his coaching career, Holtz wrote a list of names on a piece of paper—successful people on one side and not-so-successful people on the other side. He decided the difference between the two lists amounted to three things:
>
> 1) The successful ones could be trusted to do the right thing no matter how painful.

2) They were committed to excellence and tried to do their level best.

3) They cared about other people. (Leder, 100)

Gerri Leder is bringing up another interesting point here—practical reasons why we need to focus on trust, character, and integrity. Because, while all of those virtues are good in and among themselves, unless they intersect with success in business and in life, how do they relate to us? They do it in several ways:

The first is honesty. Earlier I said that if I lie, I can't necessarily remember who I lied to. This is fine for a personal philosophy, but it can be applied to a corporate philosophy as well. How many stockbrokers or investment bankers have you heard about who took the "easy" way to the top by lying and defrauding their customers? Eventually they get caught in their own webs, because lies build up, and eventually they become too much to handle. From a strictly business perspective, leaving all other considerations aside, lies are an unsustainable practice. Eventually the hens come home to roost. Just ask Bernie Madoff.

The second is trust, which is related to honesty. Chan puts it like this:

> The most common staff-retention strategies include good pay raises, attractive stock options, comprehensive training and mentoring programs, and overseas assignment opportunities. The offering of these benefits is a way of creating a bond between employees and the organization so that employees are encouraged to stay with the organization and contribute to its success. The question is, are these benefits sufficient to sustain the employer-employee bond? Although employees appreciate these benefits, they need something more to tie them to the employer. They need to feel that they can trust their employer in order to sustain an emotional bond. (22-23)

That's right—keeping your best employees happy and loyal is directly related to trust. Would you want to work for a company where you can't trust your boss? Wouldn't you rather work for a business that you can tell beyond the shadow of a doubt has the core virtues at heart?

But there are more benefits to integrating these virtues into your business philosophy. I've already told you about the importance of your company's reputation, but realness—sincerity—is also key. Simply put, people—whether ordinary Joes and Josephines or the highest pay-grade CEO you can think of—know when you're not being real with them. We sometimes fall into a trap of underestimating people, whether they are potential customers, family, or friends who we've known for years. But when we underestimate people for too long or take them for granted, we lose our respect for them and they begin to resent us. Relationships, among other things, are built on respect. If we are real with people—open and honest, giving them the benefit of the doubt—the relationships we have with them will keep being healthy and fruitful.

As a last practical consideration, I'll give you one word: differentiation. When I told you how Noah Webster defined character earlier, the second part of the definition was, "…a set of qualities that make a place or thing different from other places or things." Old-fashioned values are few and far between in today's world, whether in people's private lives or in our cutthroat business environment. Imagine the success you will have if you are able to set yourself apart from the majority of your competitors. Businesses pay hundreds of thousands of dollars to advertising agencies so they can get their name out to the public, but also so they can set themselves apart in some way. If more of them were committed to shooting straight and treating their customers and associates with respect, they probably wouldn't have to pay advertisers nearly that much. Just a thought.

Takeaways

- Friendship is based on three things—trust, character, and integrity.

- Character is the most valuable thing you have, and nobody can ever take it away.

- Relationships are the foundation for success in life. Those with strong relationship values have a better chance of succeeding in life because they have created a bigger safety net.

- The true measure of success is not measured by us, but by others.

- Integrating a moral code based on trust, integrity, and character, has a practical—not just personal—effect on businesses.

- How important is character in the relationships you are involved in and why? Think of examples of when your relationships were destroyed because of flaws in character. What could have been done to prevent those situations from deteriorating?

- After reading the chapter, what will you do in future relationships that will help bridge "the character gap?' How will that make your life more fulfilling?

Chapter Seven:

Business Relationships

While it is true that integrity and character are part of all relationships, you might wonder how they are different in a traditional business relationship. There are a couple paths to go down here in this chapter, as we can talk about business relationships or business relationships that become a mentoring experience for either party.

Here is one that worked for me, as an example. A young man signed up for my MBA class, Operational Projects. He was a successful engineer getting his master's. I had him work on a project, and the sponsor of the project was so impressed with him that he hired him as a vice president and general manager. What was interesting, in this case, was that the relationship I had with this young man started as a teacher, evolved into a mentor relationship, and although we are not in continuous contact today, it has become a business relationship, where through my manufacturer's representative's agency we have done additional business. It is funny how this relationship morphed and developed, and now any numbers of possibilities are available. Now, had we not met in class, and had I not introduced him to the client, he might not be where he is today. Again, referring to the farmer in all of us, I guess we do not know how the seeds we plant will grow and provide us with fruit and sustenance, do we?

I want to talk a little bit about traditional business relationships. Years ago, this talk about win-win relationships was all the rage, but Nancy Michaels, in a recent article for *The Huffington Post*, entitled "Reinventing Win-Win-Win Business Relationships," says that you need to ask your clients the following:

- Ask your clients what their endgame is. What do they want to accomplish? What would feel like a success to them?

- Who do they serve, and what's important to their ideal customer?

- How do they envision your services

helping them to reach or exceed their goals?

- Where have they had great success in the past?

- Are they committed to continuing to implement what's worked in the past, and open to testing new ways of communicating and servicing their clients?

When you start to ask these kinds of questions, you begin to develop a deeper win-win relationship with your clients. It is much easier when you have a client or a business owner believe that they are gaining value as part of the equation.

In order to instill that belief on their part, you have to be able to communicate the value that you can give. Communication between both parties in a business relationship is absolutely key to mutual success. Its importance can't be stressed enough.

Another key part of these questions relates to vision. One of our jobs, whether in a standard business relationship or in a mentor/protégé relationship, is to help our partners expose the vision that is already inside of them. You would be surprised at how many people have no definite idea of what they want—either out of a career, or out of their next five years, or out of their lives. Not to get too spiritual with you, here, but doesn't the Bible say something about, "Without a vision, the people perish"? I would be hard pressed to find someone who disagrees with this. Without definite goals, all we're doing is treading water, going from paycheck to paycheck, staying alive but not living for anything.

Now, how do we expose this vision that's already inside of them, just waiting to come out? Again, we do this by communicating clearly and by empathizing. We can't be effective as business partners, mentors, or coaches without walking a mile in our partners' shoes. It's important to bring up right now that we can't force our idea of what is good for our business partners or protégés onto them. We can't mistake that forcing of vision for empathizing and communication. Mentors need to break down the barriers to their protégés seeing their own visions, not supply one for them. One reason for that is because it is a lot tougher to motivate people to follow a vision that isn't truly their own. Another reason is because this kind of relationship demands respect, and forcing a vision down someone's throat does not show the respect that's necessary for a successful relationship. Lois Zachary and Lory Fischler put it like this:

> Although both mentor and mentee must play active roles in the goal-setting process, the responsibility for facilitating it lies with the mentor. The mentor's role is to ensure that the mentee's goals fit within the framework of workplace reality, as well as the mentee's capability and talent. Goal setting should be driven by the mentee. ("Facilitating Mentee-Driven Goal Setting." 76)

This is a key area in which business partnerships differ from mentor/protégé relationships. Whereas in a mentor/protégé relationship, the mentor is aiding the protégé to achieve his/her goals, in a business partnership, the goal setting is not driven by your business partner alone, but by both of you; otherwise, it wouldn't be much of a partnership. But respect is still very important to the relationship. They need to respect your vision, and you need to respect theirs. Katherine Reynolds Lewis, in "5 Mentor Mistakes to Avoid," writes, "When you ask someone to give you advice, you owe the courtesy of respecting their time and making the most of it… Play an active role in the relationship." We can maintain true partnerships by being active and encouraging activity in our partners. Being equally invested in the project at hand is one of the keys to respect.

But, as Susan Berfield points out in "Mentoring Can Be Messy," "Respect isn't enough, though. Ideally, both people know what they want out of the arrangement," (80). This brings up an important point—most business and mentor/protégé relationships need a specific direction or goal in order to be successful, at least at first. Little puts it this way:

> The benefits to both parties may also be the reason why many mentoring relationships endure long after the expected period of time…the key to a long-term relationship is one that is appreciated by both parties: "If you can find value and rapport in what they are doing, the mentoring can continue for the whole career of that person." (27)

A mentor/protégé relationship does not necessarily need to continue on a long term basis—it can change its nature, just like the example I told you about earlier in this chapter, where I started as a teacher, became a mentor, and moved on to being a business associate—but in order for it to be counted as a success, both parties need to benefit from it in some way. Kate Vitasek and Joseph Tillman, in "Creating Personal Accountability in Mentoring Relationships," phrase it like this:

> I write that any vested relationship flourishes best in a culture in which participants work together to ensure their mutual success. In its simplest form, being vested is a mindset in which two or more parties build on each other's strengths to create and develop something better. (36)

Being vested in people implies being committed to them and to the relationship. The temptation may be to begin a business or mentor relationship with someone who thinks similarly to you—someone who you get along with personally, and who you feel comfortable around. This is a temptation that you should avoid. Business relationships can be so powerful precisely because both parties are very good at different aspects of the work. Lewis, talking about mentor relationships, though what she says is just as applicable to business relationships, says a couple of things about this: "Similarly, your mentors shouldn't all be former supervisors. Pick people who have exposure to a different business area or even those in a different company or sector of your industry," ("5 Mentor Mistakes to Avoid"), and "It may be comfortable to develop a relationship with a mentor with a background similar to yours. That's not the way to grow. Instead, seek out a mentor with a different experience and perspective, one who can help you identify blind spots," (same). The goal in any business relationship is success, and to succeed we need to find ways to grow. Growing is not always easy, and sometimes we get growing pains—but growing is always worth it. The short-term vulnerability and uncomfortableness we may feel around someone we wouldn't naturally associate with is tiny compared to the potential benefits of the relationship.

Another area of potential discomfort for us in a business or mentor/protégé relationship is willingness to accept advice and other opinions from our associates. Sometimes our protégés might actually be able to teach us something, or they might be more experienced in a certain area than we are. When this happens, we have to be able to accept it and not have a knee-jerk reaction that we know everything. This comes down to being open to keep the channels of communication flowing, and it comes back to mutual respect. Protégés need to know that we respect them as much as we need to know that they respect us, and if we are willing to learn and be humble in these instances, the relationships can only prosper and grow. The times that we can learn from our associates are actually one of the benefits for us in relationships of this sort. We are enriching others because of the experience we can give them, and we are becoming enriched ourselves—win-win.

What about for the protégé or the business partner? What benefits are they getting, besides our experience? Tracy puts it this way: "By going to people who are ahead of you and opening yourself to their input and guidance, you save yourself the years it would take and the thousands of dollars it would cost you to learn what you need to learn by yourself. This is the essence of mentoring relationships," (4). If we could monetize the value of what our protégés or business associates are getting, the worth would probably be too high to pay. We shouldn't forget that what they are bringing to the table is also of value to us, even though sometimes it forces us to think differently and change our plans.

But that is the point! The goal of every relationship should be to make the parties involved more successful, and success comes through growth and adaptation. Adaptation is vastly important for survival. Writing about this, Chan says,

> Change brings opportunities but can also be quite unsettling. Although we cannot control every change, we can control the way we perceive, adapt to, and utilize change. It calls for the ability to be open-minded, flexible, innovative, and proactive and to maintain steadfastness in the face of a crisis. If organizations want to have an edge in the increasingly competitive business environment, they should consider paying more attention to these qualities when recruiting, training, retaining, and mentoring staff. (19)

In today's business environment, we are either moving forward or we are moving backward; we're either swimming or we're sinking. The world is changing too fast for us not to change with it—if we want to be successful. Here's what Green says about it: "In today's hyper-fast markets, strategic agility – the ability to move fast with focus and flexibility – is an essential leadership skill that enables your organization to stay on track when circumstances change beyond your control," (21). If this sounds daunting, realize that this is why we have partners, mentors, and protégés in the first place—all with different strengths than us. We grow individually when we're willing to accept wisdom and life lessons wherever we can get them, and we bring all of the things we've learned back to the companies we represent. Change comes from individuals. The title of this book is *Growing Comes from Planting Seeds*, and that refers to the mentorship process, but it can also refer to how change starts with the individual.

So adaptability requires us to try new things and accept wisdom from sometimes-unlikely places, but it also requires us to stay loose. Kilkelly writes, "Plans and processes are important, but it is even more important to work with people and through people to allow the organization to evolve on a constant basis to meet new challenges and opportunities." If our plans are too rigid, they will break when pressure is applied to them. Other people—and other perspectives—are the answer to our ideas becoming too rigid. When we understand this concept, and we don't take offense when our business partners give us ideas that might not sit well with us at first, then we will be on the road to a dynamic, adaptable, and successful endeavor.

Takeaways

- Finding out your clients' or business partners' goals and visions is important to making the relationship work.

- Clear communication and empathy are vital to the mentoring process.

- Each partner needs to respect the vision of the other.

- Most business and mentor/protégé relationships need a specific direction or goal in order to be successful, at least at first.

- Adaptability requires us to try new things and accept wisdom from sometimes-unlikely places, but it also requires us to stay loose.

- Think of a good business relationship and why it was successful. Did it follow the "win-win" principle? Could it have benefitted both parties differently had other techniques been used?

- Think of a relationship that didn't quite work. Can you explain why it did not? Looking back, if you had tried other techniques, would it have succeeded?

- Can you think of a business relationship that taught you a lot? What did you learn and how did it affect you or your performance?

Chapter Eight:

Influencing without Authority

I always thought this was a great topic, and of course, it makes a good study to look at influence and just how it affects relationships and/or people's reactions to those relationships, favorably or negatively. Influencing happens irrespective of having authority over another individual or not. I had lunch with a CEO of a major industrial organization and he told me, "I understand how the dynamics have changed over the past twenty years. Twenty years ago we manufactured most of what we made in our plants and the operational folks from those plants had full Profit & Loss responsibility. Today we outsource most of what we sell and manufacture just a small part of our product, but our operations folks are still responsible for the P&L, rather than the supply chain folks, who are in control of the outsourcing programs." This is exactly the reason we all need to learn to influence without authority.

Those people in the organization that learn how to influence people that don't work for them build an undercurrent that allows them to be far more successful in their roles. They get far more done because they utilize the resources of other departments and people within their influence. Because of this they can also build a pretty impressive list of allies and can become very persuasive. Don't underestimate yourself either, as many folks will say to themselves, "What could I possibly have that someone else wants?" The answer would probably surprise them.

In Cohen and Bradford's book, *Influence without Authority*, they state that you not only need to understand your desires and wants, but also the needs and wants of the person you are trying to influence (90). If you can see clearly what you want now, you should be able to focus on what the other person wants, as well and create a mutually beneficial equation. Does this sound familiar? It should, since I've been going on about it at length. Seeing the needs and wants of the people we are trying to influence is called empathy, and it is absolutely crucial for anyone in a leadership position. Along with that comes having your own vision, which I've also talked about. We have to make sure of our own desires and goals before we are qualified to influence others concerning these.

One of the other key parts of influencing, according to Cohen and Bradford, is understanding that relationships matter. Anybody that tells you otherwise is dead wrong. That is why, in a number of areas within this book, you hear me refer to trust. Trust is a key basis in developing the relationship. Cohen and Bradford say, "In any circumstance, good, open, and trusting relationships have a number of benefits."

Other benefits of trust, according to Cohen and Bradford, include the following:

- Communication is more complete, so you are more likely to know the needs and currencies of the other person.

- The other person is more likely to take your word and be open to being influenced.

- You can pay back later in a wider range of currencies and less exactly.

- Personal currencies where there is connection become more important, which broadens the kind of currencies you can pay in.

These personal currencies, according to Cohen and Bradford, are the medium of exchange in relationships. They are not actual money, but they are of intrinsic value, nonetheless. These could include a series of favors that you do for a co-worker, who later returns these favors; or maybe an impromptu lunch where you find you have more in common with a co-worker than you previously thought; or they could be as simple as a great conversation with someone at your company. These personal currencies are made all the time, and you may find that over time they develop into something just as valuable as the money in your paycheck.

For this reason, it's important for us to remember to not burn our bridges easily. Yes, there are times in life when we have to end our relationships with people—whether that's because they continually take advantage of us, or the relationship has become unhealthy in some way, or for some other reason—but if at all possible, we should avoid the temptation to do this. Sure, there are times at work where we will want to end our relationship with other, usually-valued co-workers, but at these times it's important to really examine why we are upset, and then work to either calm ourselves down or try to communicate with them calmly why they have hurt us.

How we handle disagreements silently shows others the caliber of our character, which in turn does wonders for our effectiveness as influencers, and shows our capabilities as leaders.

Dave Stachowiak recently posted on LinkedIn his rules for influencing without authority: "I get this question almost weekly: 'How can I hold someone accountable that doesn't report to me?' Even if you can't dictate compliance, you can get enthusiastic cooperation. Here are eight ways you can – and why this kind of influence is better than mere compliance."

His comments are below:

> 1**) Stop wishing for control:** If you think being someone's manager will make things easier, think again. Take someone to lunch who manages people and ask them what it's like to be able to tell people what to do. When they stop laughing, they'll probably tell you it's even harder in management.
>
> 2) **Move beyond compliance:** Sure, managers can get compliance, but effective managers' bark orders as a last resort. Think back to the best manager you've had…it's doubtful they were in your face much. Rather, they probably created an environment where you wanted to take action. That should be your goal.

3) **Care:** If all you know about the other party is what they can do for you, you're missing the foundation of influence. We're all human – and most of us give attention to those who show interest. Find out something they enjoy unrelated to work and ask about it. Demonstrate that you care – and mean it.

4**) Offer to help:** Almost every good team I know relies on influence over authority. Start by spending one extra hour a week helping out others with a deadline. Do it for a while – and demonstrate that you're a team player. People will help if you've helped them.

5**) Set expectations:** Just because you aren't the manager doesn't mean that you can't make agreements. Approach people before it's a crisis. Tell them what you need and what it will take. Be realistic on commitments (nobody likes a bait-and-switch). Ask how you can make it easier. Try to make it beneficial for them too.

6) **Thank people in public:** When someone takes time to help, thank them. Maybe mention it at the next staff meeting – or thank them in an email and copy their manager/team. Virtually nobody takes the time to do this genuinely, so people notice.

7**) Be real:** I've had times in my career when I've approached a colleague and said, "I need your help. It's going to take time, will bore you to tears, will never help your career, and you'll get absolutely nothing except my thanks. Interested?" They usually laugh, and we figure it out. People like honesty – and humor.

8) **Swim with champions:** Yeah, I know there's that one troll that won't help you even if you did all of the above. Engage them when you have to, but invest real time with people who also care and want to grow their careers too. You'll raise each other up.

You see, there are common threads in all of these philosophies. Note how many principles remain the same, whether you are mentoring, coaching, or building the business relationship. Within all of these you will find it very helpful to be able to influence without authority as well. Consider just how many times you are dealing with someone in another department, someone you don't know very well or not at all. Consider just how many times your boss comes to you with a task, which if managed correctly, and if you are to be successful with a solution, means you have to get others to buy in to the concept. Isn't it great to influence, and while influencing, build mentoring or coaching relationships, and enhance your business relationships as well?

Another thing I'd like to mention about influencing before switching gears is this: Influencing is not forcing. I said this earlier, but it's important enough to mention again. When you truly understand the needs of a person you are interacting with, you don't have to force anything. This does not mean that people won't sometimes have to be persuaded, because sometimes people don't know what they want, or they're unwilling to do what it takes to get what they want. This is why it's important to know exactly what it takes to influence people in whatever situation we find ourselves in.

Further, in order to influence, we have to know how to use every tool at our disposal. This is why I keep mentioning trust and communication. Getting others to buy into our vision means communicating to them effectively so it can become their vision, too. But even if they see our vision and don't trust us, we've still failed. This is why Michael Beck, in "Core Competencies," says, "Leadership is more about *who you are* than about *what you know or what you do*," (6). Ultimately, we lead—and influence—by example. Influencing is a lifelong project; it is the practical upshot of all that we've talked about so far—character, integrity, trust, and reputation.

Like it or not, if we desire to be influencers, our lives will be open to scrutiny. People want leadership, but they want more than that, too—they want GOOD leadership.

The importance of being able to tell a story

I had to include this under the influencing without authority chapter because I think it is directly tied to influencing others. Now, some have called me too folksy—in my writing and my mannerisms—and I suppose at times I am too folksy, but I think sometimes the way you tell a story has a lot to do with the way folks receive that story. I think it is important to be able to put yourselves in someone's shoes if you are going to be able to relate to them, and I choose to do it by telling stories. When you tell a story, you leave it up to someone's imagination as to whether they fit in it or not and they find meaning in your story. It's funny, but one young student I am mentoring dropped me a note and told me he will keep me apprised of *his story*. He is referring to the first time he and I met, and I asked him to tell me *"his story'*.

Stories can influence others as well, either directly or indirectly. Stories have a way of sinking into our subconscious mind and creating different feelings for different people, but while still creating a common bond. The story, whether we like it or not, creates a bond, evokes a memory either good or bad that the subconscious resurrects at an appropriate time for us to use, however we see fit. Everyone can fit themselves or someone they know into a story, and I believe that this makes a difference in how people perceive you. Include stories in your proposal to influence others and you will find they will serve your purpose very well. Stories will make you more engaging, too, and that is what we are striving for as we try and build trusting relationships as mentors.

Storytelling is another hot topic today. Whenever I speak, one of the things people often ask is, “Can you teach me how to tell a story?” I have to say, this is easier said than done. Stories have to be adapted, and you have to really be able to think on your feet. Stories always have to serve to reinforce our points and highlight a statement we have just made.

The best way in my mind to get your point across and reinforce that point is to tell a story. Tell a story that relates to the point you just made that will reinforce that point with the person you are communicating with. What I have found is that many times folks won't remember the specific point you made by itself, but because they find great relevance in the story, they will remember the story, and then they will remember the point you were trying to drive home. It's interesting how our minds work isn't it? That is why it is important to store the stories in your mind for future use. It is really a key piece to store in your arsenal of communicative abilities. Believe me, it will distinguish you from the others and make you a far better communicator than you ever thought possible.

Some practical considerations to keep in mind while telling a story: First, this might sound stupid, but know the point that you're trying to make before you start telling your story. I know a young man who really enjoys telling stories, and he tells them entertainingly enough, but sometimes he trails off near the end and says, "I don't know where I was going with that." Now, the end is what people stay for, and if you don't have anything of value for your listeners to take away at the end, they soon won't be listeners.

Second: Know how to tell a story without getting sidetracked. If people wanted to hear somebody going off on tangents and telling funny observations about life, they'd go see a comedian. This is not to say that you can't be funny in the stories you tell—people generally like someone with a good sense of humor—but it is to tell you that the people listening to you in a workplace environment are listening to you for the bottom line.

Third: Don't ramble on and on. Phrases like "Keep it pithy"and "short and sweet" come to mind at the moment. People will listen to your stories—up to a point—but their time is valuable, and they have to get the impression that you know that. People, and I'm including myself here, are judging all the time, for good or bad. It's just what we do—it's a survival mechanism, and no matter what we might say about stereotyping, we probably recognize that usually it's a pretty helpful trait to have. We make up our minds about people, sometimes in the first few seconds we know them. This is why first impressions are so important. You don't want to be that guy or lady who everyone knows as "the rambler," or "the side tracker," or "the pointless one." Mark Twain, in his usual witty way, had this to say about it: "It's better to keep your mouth shut and appear stupid than open it and remove all doubt."

Fourth: Finally, practice makes perfect. Are you quiet because you don't enjoy speaking in public? Do you get nervous in group settings? Does the thought of entertaining someone with a personal story intimidate you? Practice. Practice in front of a mirror, practice in a car, practice wherever it suits you—but by all means, practice. If this thought seems silly to you, ask yourself, "whoever got better at something by doing nothing about it?" If developing relationships with people and getting better at speaking to groups of co-workers is something you value, then how will your situation change unless you practice?

Takeaways

- Influencing people who don't work for you allows you to be far more successful in your role.

- Influencing is not forcing. Don't try to foist your vision onto your protégé or partner.

- The ability to tell engaging, entertaining stories is one of the best ways to get your point across, and reinforce it, too.

- The more you can take a story and relate it to your listener, the better off you are. Always try to tie the story into something your listener can relate to.

- People love to hear stories, but the stories have to have meaning for the listener. So listen to those signals they are giving you and tell the appropriate and meaningful story for the situation.

Exercises

- Think about your particular ways of influencing people. Do some of these ways rub off on others the wrong way? Could you up your influencing game in one or more areas? What more could you add to your influencing "toolset" to start influencing people around you in the most effective ways?

- Just for a moment, think about the great learning experiences you have had in life. Now think about the circumstances surrounding those moments of clarity. What are the stories? Think about how to connect what you have learned in the past and the stories attached to those moments, and now think about how you can bring those stories into day-to-day life in order to help people around you.

Chapter Nine:

Relationships that Last a Lifetime

Mentoring relationships have no expiration date; they have no ties binding the mentor and the protégé together. Sometimes they last a short time, and sometimes they last forever. Mentoring is always relationship driven. It typically provides a safe haven for protégés to hone and develop their skills. They can share successes and failures with their mentors without any repercussions. They can objectively look at the experiences they have both gone through, and the mentor can offer great advice. This relationship typically then becomes more personal, and it sometimes includes work/life balance issues and self-confidence issues that aren't typical in the coaching environment.

This might seem all well and good, in a perfect world, but how do we ensure that this ideal, judgment-free relationship can happen in the sometimes-cutthroat world of business? Who among high-potential employees doesn't have a story of someone who has stepped on their toes or held them back in order to get promoted or become recognized in some other way? Sharing things with someone else without repercussions might sound a little impractical, but there are ways to ensure that this judgment-free ideal can be realized. First, we go back to what Lewis said about mentors, that we should pick them from different departments of our businesses, or even different companies or sectors of our industries. The point here is to make competitiveness between mentor and protégé a non-issue, because mentors are more experienced in business and generally do not want what their protégés have.

Another practical way to make a mentor/protégé relationship start off on the right foot from day one is mentioned by Max Messmer, in "Building an Effective Mentoring Program": "Privacy and trust are essential to a successful mentoring program, so confidentiality guidelines should be established up-front. Protégés are more likely to ask questions and seek assistance from their mentors if they know there won't be negative career implications," (P 18). If it sounds a little weird to you that you should make confidentiality guidelines up-front, think of the benefits to both parties, and also remember that mentor relationships can be friendships, but they are not just friendships. Between professionals, guidelines are not only acceptable, but they are also the reasonable thing to do. This is not to say that the relationship has to be grounded on something so formal as a contract, but that the "rules" should be established very early on in a way that both parties understand.

Being a content expert is not as important to the mentor and protégé because both are exploring the softer side of issues, such as problems in the workplace and personal considerations. All can be accomplished in the mentoring relationship. Mentoring is development driven. There does not have to be a measurement system in place for mentoring. And yet, there are some studies that Beverly Crowell and Beverly Kay remind us of in their article, "Build Your DREAM Team." Among these are, "...one of the top five reasons employees stay engaged at work is the opportunity for career growth, learning and development," and, "The cost of replacing talented employees can average as much as two-three times that employee's annual salary," and that, "...actively disengaged employees cost the United States over $300 billion a year on lost productivity," and finally, "People with mentors are twice as likely to stay inside an organization – stay longer and produce more," (19). So while we do not need to have metrics in place to show us that a particular mentoring relationship is being successful in one or more areas, we do have a larger picture of mentoring programs having proven track records, both personally and for the bottom lines of the companies in which they take place.

And, although we probably are already convinced of mentoring's personal benefits, Jayson Forrest, in "Mentoring Makes it Easy," reminds us that, "At the heart of any successful career is the personal satisfaction that comes from doing a great job that you enjoy doing. Fundamental to this is the opportunity of being mentored by someone more experienced..." (18). Sometimes the "softer sides" of issues are more important than individual projects, because they provide the protégé with the foundational philosophy he or she needs to be effective for their entire life. Fulfillment at work is one of these issues, but it is so important for anyone who wants to have a long, successful, and happy career.

Contrasted with the sometimes lofty and personal ambitions of mentoring, coaching is typically task oriented and more down to earth. For example, the defensive line coach is going to coach you to aggressively go after the quarterback for a sack. Or the corporate coach is going to coach you in achieving superior numbers within your business realm. Coaching is done for as long as the coach and the coached have the relationship, and it is always performance driven. There are metrics to measure the success of the relationship. Are you successful or not? In business coaching you possibly can measure by a ROI (Return on Investment); skill and knowledge are much more easily tested.

Business relationships can either turn into friendships when the business relationship expires or has run its course, or they can simply cease to exist. Now, if the relationship is one of mentoring (a business partner), of course mentoring still takes precedence, and the mentoring relationship, of course, continues.

In many of these cases, relationships can last a period of time. Coaching typically lasts for the shortest amount of time, limited as it is to a defined period, and when you've been coached and you've achieved the result, there is no need for the coach anymore, unless it has developed into a mentoring relationship, which could very well happen, especially if the relationship turns into one that develops mutual respect. There needs to be a clear end to the coaching program as well, with an appropriate transitioning process to manage the end of the relationship.

Typically, mentor relationships will last the longest. Again, because the relationship consists of an extended period of time and there are fewer walls and fewer constraints, many of these relationships will last a lifetime. I will give you an example about one mentoring relationship I have had for over fifteen years. It started when the young man worked for me, continued when he decided to go to school for his master's degree, went on to his move to Europe, as well as his wedding in Europe, his emigration to the US, and the birth of his children. All along, he has asked and sought out my advice and counsel on life's most important career and personal issues, and I imagine the relationship will continue through his middle aged years and my senior years. The benefits to both parties may also be the reason many mentoring relationships endure long after the expected period of time. The key to a long lasting relationship is it being one that is appreciated by both parties. Again we come back to what Kerry Little said: "If you can find value and rapport in what they are doing, the mentoring can continue for the whole career of that person," (27).

One of the key words in this quote that you might have overlooked is "can." A mentoring relationship *can* continue for the whole career. It doesn't have to. I'm not saying this to make you depressed, because we all want productive, healthy relationships that benefit both parties—I'm saying it because I don't want you to beat yourself up if your particular mentoring relationship doesn't happen that way. We all have a thought in our heads about what our perfect situations will look like, and we might be guilty of pressuring ourselves to make them turn out that way, even if our personalities and our mentors' or protégés' personalities aren't suited to that dynamic.

Remember this: people aren't perfect. There will always be problems, even in the best relationships. Don't judge the success of your relationship by the problems it contains. We can't get caught in the trap of letting our vision of what we think a mentor/protégé relationship should look like get in the way of what ours will actually end up looking like. We have to let our relationships evolve naturally, and take them as they come, and not put too high of expectations on ourselves if they are not exactly as we envisioned.

So you don't become best friends with your mentor? No one said you have to be. Your mentor is there to help you, and the friendship is a bonus. The relationship is not a failure as long as it is producing benefits for you. If your mentor can't help you in a specific area, that's all right, because he is probably able to help you in another area.

Now, this leads us to a tricky subject: what happens when a mentor can't teach you anymore? In an ideal case, this happens because the mentor has taught you everything she can about her subject, and she has done so in a way that lets you know you have an ally and a friend for life. In this type of example, the relationship then evolves to a place where both of you are still able to benefit from each other, but more through your individualized experiences of what you go through at your separate businesses or departments, and not so much through a student/teacher dynamic. We can always learn through other peoples' experiences, because other peoples' experiences are different than ours—even if we have the benefit of more degrees, or more years in the field, or a higher position in the company.

But what happens if a "mentor" can't teach you anymore, or was never able to help you? This is where the situation gets less than ideal. In this situation, there are a few questions you can ask yourself in order to try to fix the problem.

The first of these is to ask yourself, what went wrong? Knowing as objectively as possible what happened is normally a very good idea when you're trying to salvage a relationship. If you know the problem, you're able to fix it better than you would be otherwise.

If you are the mentor in the relationship, it is important for you to ask yourself what your protégé wanted out of the process that you could not, or were not willing to provide. This might require an open and honest conversation that could get uncomfortable at points, but if the relationship still has a chance to be salvaged, open and honest conversations are what's called for. By saying open and honest, I do not mean insulting and destructive. As professional adults, we can tell others what we need from them that we are not getting, and they can tell us what they need from us and are not getting, without the situation devolving into a fight. Maintaining our professionalism is key when a situation goes south, and as long as we keep the situation civil, we have a good chance of working through it.

After we have had this open and honest discussion and we have determined what went wrong to set the relationship on its current course, we need to determine a corrective action. This could be as simple as an apology from one member of the party to the other. It could mean that both of you work out an alternate game plan, or establish another goal that had slipped your mind before, or come up with a different way of relating to each other.

The bottom line is, if the relationship can be saved, save it. No matter how much work it takes to bring the relationship back to a healthy area, it will not be as much work as finding someone else willing to be mentored or to mentor, establishing trust with them, and coming to a place where you are able to relate to each other easily and friendlily.

No matter how much we might hate it, sometimes relationships have to end, whether that's because one party is not suited for the other, or because we find that their mentoring philosophy is immoral, or because their advice is just plain wrong. When this happens we owe it to ourselves to be professional in this also. When reputations are at stake, how we handle the ends of relationships can be just as important as how we handle the relationships themselves.

Takeaways

- The mentor/protégé relationship needs to be a judgment-free zone. Protégés have to be able to share successes and failures with their mentors without any repercussions.

- Privacy and trust are essential to a successful mentoring program, so confidentiality guidelines should be established up-front.

- There will always be problems, even in the best relationships.

- Mentoring is a selfless proposition. The protégé comes first, always.

- The mentor needs to be ego-less when it comes to protégé. These types of relationships will last forever. But remember, this takes a special mentor.

- Since mentor/protégé relationships are not all about business, think about a way that the relationship can expand outside of a business setting. What might you bond with a potential mentor or protégé about? Mutual interests? Common experiences? How would you personally go about making the relationship as strong as possible?

- Have you ever been in a relationship and found that the other party was not satisfied with what you could provide? What could you have done to change this, if anything? Now think about if you were the one who was not satisfied. What were your reasons for being that way?

Chapter Ten:

The Mentor Matrix

I believe in visuals. In my book, *The Dysfunctional Organization*, I said that the way people learn today is by doing, not by reading, and that is one of the major reasons our MBAs fail us. So I thought, what better way to describe the differences between mentors, coaches, and business relationships than to show them in a concise and well thought-out and laid-out form?

Hence the Mentor Matrix was born. I wanted to be able and sit down and talk about all of the variables between mentoring, coaching, and developing a business relationship, and how they were different, so I started the Mentor Matrix. It is meant to be expanded and developed, particularly as you try the various techniques and exercises we describe in this book. It is not meant to be all encompassing, because each situation is different and has different variables. It is meant, however, to provide you with the framework of telling just how mentoring is different from being coached, and just how that is different from a business relationship—because there are differences, as you can imagine, and as we have described in this book. So mark up the pages and expand as you use this as your journey along mentorship.

I tested this out on a talk I did with a group of professionals I spoke to at a conference and they all seem to relate to the differences. In fact, as we went through this, we had the opportunity to expand it quite a bit. I started to highlight what I thought were important differentiators throughout the entire process, and that might give you a taste for where to start, but where you end up is entirely up to you. Either way, it will help you visually see that mentoring and coaching—though they have similar traits—are very different in context, but they also have some traits that are applicable in developing business relationships as well.

The Mentor Matrix can also help you with stating goals, with clearing up any confusion about what kind of situation you may be in, and with showing you what might be missing from your existing mentor, coaching, or business relationship. Use it and change it according to your own individual needs, but do consider it a tool to help you identify exactly where you are and what you might be missing from your current arrangement.

The Mentor Matrix

Developed as part of *Growing Comes from Planting Seeds*

Coaching

Key party: team

Coach does what is right for the group (team)

Somewhat guarded thinking

Coach invests in team's success Individual secondary; team is primary measure of success

Shorter term process means quicker benefits

Limited variables at play

Business Relationships

Key party: all participants

Has to be right for all parties

Don't trust partner right away—only after significant time

Relationship is shorter process

Many variables at play

Mentoring

Key party: protégé

Mentor selfless—only needs to be right for protégé

Emotional intelligence

Mentor invests in protégé's success

Openness and honesty

Critical thinking

Trust not an issue—mentor comfortable in own skin

Long term process; relationships last longest

No variables at play

Chapter Eleven:

Competencies in the Relationship

There are certain competencies that are required in any relationship. As humans, we have certain expectations for the people we interact with on a daily basis, and if the people around us don't meet these, we get disappointed. Magnified as they are in the mentor relationship, people not meeting these expectations becomes more than just getting let down, it becomes the difference between a successful and unsuccessful partnership. Siobhan Rogers, in "Mentoring for Change: Adding value where it counts," says regarding this: "For the mentor relationship to be successful, it is important to assess whether the mentor has the skills, competence, qualities and time to dedicate to a mentoring relationship," (8). This might sound unfair, that the success of the relationship depends on the mentor, but the mentor has the experience, and is therefore the dominant party in the relationship. It would be unfair to put most of the weight on the protégé.

Let's get into some specific requirements now, starting with mentors. Earlier in the book I talked about some of the competencies that are required by mentors. I mentioned things like we are all empowered with various gifts, which undoubtedly includes mentoring. Not all of us have the mentoring gift—some of us might be fine businessmen or salesmen, and we might just not be blessed with the patience that can sometimes be required in a mentoring relationship. Don't beat yourself up over this, if so. This is a gift that can sometimes be learned, so definitely try to obtain it, but you might find that you're more effective in other areas after you've given it a fair shot a few times.

I've also mentioned the leadership and support that mentors must give their protégés. This is no joke—when we become mentors we take on a responsibility, and our protégés look to us for advice and practical wisdom. If we are not willing to provide that, we should seriously reconsider our attitudes and our commitments. If one of our "strengths" is actually a kind of toughness that prohibits meaningful relationships, we should listen to Jerry Frantz, who in "Why Advisers and Mentors Matter," says, "Many executives are take-charge by nature. But one of the qualities of an ideal mentor includes the ability to be a good coach and listener, which is a powerful and effective way of approaching leadership — one that has its own rewards," (18). We may just find that we need to approach leadership in a different way in order to support those we mentor. We may just find that this reexamination of our guiding principles is exactly what we needed.

Some other things I mentioned earlier were the virtues that a mentor must possess—virtues like your starting point being one of loving people, and being wise, caring, and compassionate. These might seem like basic human qualities that we should all strive for—and we should—but sometimes it's hard to muster compassion and wisdom when we're stressed after a long week of work, where everyone seemingly has been taking part of us and not giving anything back. At these times, putting aside our stress and need for some kind of break for the sake of our protégés might be one of the most difficult things we could imagine. And yet we do it, because the mentor/protégé relationship is a serious commitment, and the development of our protégés will be one of the most fulfilling parts of our legacies.

So, leaving behind the question of moral integrity for a second, the competencies required by the mentor, in order to be successful, are centered on compatibility. I think both parties need to be able to get along, and they need to have, or be able to cultivate, respect for each other. This starts with the mentor being, well, competent. This comes first and foremost because no one will respect you or join in a productive, long-term relationship with you unless you know what you're talking about. Now, you might think that this is a non-issue, because how would a person get to the position of being a mentor if he doesn't know what he's talking about, but businesses sometimes don't make the best decisions when promoting people. (If you want to know more about that, read my first book, *The Dysfunctional Organization*, where I talk about that issue at length.) My point about competency here is that businesses might make poor decisions about the people they put into positions of authority, but on a personal level, the protégé will be able to tell.

In almost all cases the mentor has something that the protégé wants, be it knowledge, “the keys to knowledge and/or success,” or career success. The mentor has to be trustworthy and has to consider (even though this rarely happens) that the protégé may test him sometimes to see where his or her allegiances lie. The mentor also has to be able to push the protégé to extremes the protégé never thought possible, and to push for extreme results. That is the value of having a mentor. This has to be a give and take relationship, again, being honest with each other, and the protégé has to be able to talk to the mentor as to why a particular strategy or idea could or couldn’t possibly work. There has to be a keen sense of who each other is in this process. For example, the protégé has to be open enough to discuss why a particular approach has failed and be able to learn from it; and the mentor has to be able to lay out all options or solutions and let the protégé have some flexibility in dealing with whatever he or she thinks the appropriate options are.

I like to tell the story of one of my protégés who decided not to take my advice. As he did this, I told him, "I understand, you are a big boy now and can make that decision yourself." (I am fortunate that I can talk to my protégés that way, as it lends a little humor and creates an even tighter bond.) So when he failed, I used this as an opportunity not to rub his face in it, but as a learning experience for him, saying, "OK. We tried it your way. Now let's try it my way and see if we get the same result." It was successful, and he learned a very valuable lesson that day. And oh, by the way, so did I. I learned just how much the protégé was willing to listen and how much he trusted me, and now he knows I look out for his interests above all, and we have built this great trusting relationship.

The other thing mentors need to understand is that the protégé does not have to copy your style. Every person has their own unique way of doing things, and that is what keeps the old world going 'round, as they say. The mentor has to understand that the protégé is taking in influences from all around him, and he emulates little pieces of all those influencers to create his own style. Our job as mentors is not so much about style as it is substance. Try it next time—pay attention to how the protégé engages with other influences and see just what she picks up and emulates. Don't be discouraged if they don't emulate you, as you are still offering a very valuable service to the protégé. And oh, by the way, you are the most influential influencer they have because; you are helping your protégés pull it all together.

Both parties in the relationship need to hold each other accountable for the success or failure of the task. Dialogue needs to occur when one party feels slighted, or feels that the other party isn't listening, or more likely, doesn't understand exactly what the other is trying to communicate. Practically speaking, dialogue is one of those things that absolutely cannot happen unless there is trust, honesty, and openness between the parties. Even when we disagree with our mentor or our protégé, we still have to trust them enough to put our concerns out in the open, rather than letting those concerns become resentments and start to eat away at us.

The mentor needs to have great listening capability and be willing to not interrupt, even when the solution is obvious to the mentor. Give the protégé time to speak their mind about the issues and see if they end up talking themselves into a solution. The mentor needs to listen on a number of levels—physically, emotionally, intellectually, and intuitively. There may be subtle messages the protégé is giving the mentor by what they say or how they communicate, and the mentor has to be able to pick up on those subtleties. While picking up on those various issues, the mentor should not be thinking of solutions, but of learning outcomes for the protégé. You see, it is not about proving you are right and that the protégé is wrong, but it is about developmentally fixing the problem. It's like the saying, "you can lead a horse to water, but you can't make him drink." You, the mentor, have to use your intelligence to get the protégé to be willing to recognize the water and want to drink it as well—because it is nourishment—and make the protégé whole. The mentor also has to be able to know when the lesson has been learned and the protégé is ready to move on. Can the protégé demonstrate the skill necessary to move onward to other issues and tasks? And lastly, the mentor needs to be articulate enough—without being condescending—to talk about what the protégé just learned in that valuable lesson.

Let's switch tracks now and talk a little bit about the competencies required by the protégé, because, while a protégé's role in the relationship may not be as important to its success as the mentor's, it is still very important. The protégé or leadership candidate must be worth your time. Sure, as the mentor, part of that also falls on you—your ability to see his or her raw talent—but there are few things worse than investing in a new employee or a young person from outside the company, only to find that they don't have the will or the work ethic to do what they need to do to become successful.

Hagemann and Stoope call protégés "High Potentials," which is a good reminder of why we are in the mentoring relationship in the first place. We want those who we are mentoring to recognize their potential and develop the tools to reach it. But they cannot reach that mindset without a few critical tools. Hagemann and Stoope write, "High potentials who want to make it to the "suite seats" are expected to deliver results, be inspiring leaders, think critically, be flexible, innovative, collaborative AND be able to lead influentially," (18). If these traits sound familiar, it's because they are what is expected to be found in mentors. Protégés are mentors in training. Their success is our success. This is why successful mentoring relationships give us so much fulfillment.

Hagemann also write concerning protégés that:

> Asking a high potential to bring his A-Game every day, doesn't mean that he or she will

> never make a mistake. Many mistakes will be made and that is all a part of the learning. It also doesn't mean that he or she can never rest. In fact, rest and pacing is required. What it does mean is that the high potential no longer allows him/her to let down the guard. 19

Holding the high potential protégé up to a higher standard is one of the toughest, yet most rewarding parts of his or her training. We have to allow for human error, because this happens to the best of us, and we have to know when to stop pushing, but we do have to let our protégés know that they are in this relationship with the sole goal of excellence. Half measures don't cut it. "Good enoughs" don't cut it. It's like the founder of Lego, Ole Kirk Christiansen, said: "Only the best is good enough." Whether we're working at a toy manufacturer or a stock brokerage, excellence should always be our motto.

One last point about the competencies expected in a protégé: pure talent alone does not cut it. Nine times out of ten, give me the person who works hard at everything he does, rather than the person who is a genius in a certain area and knows it. Assuming that you are working with a protégé who is a hard worker and doesn't expect everything to be handed to him, keep this formula by Clinton Longenecker in mind:

> Performance = ability x motivation x support.
>
> Anyone's performance can be viewed as a function of this critical equation and is central to the practice of effective coaching. Ability is the employee's skills and talents in effectively performing their job. Motivation is the employee's level of inner drive and work ethic in performing their job. Support is providing the employee with the information, tools, and the resources necessary to perform their job. (34)

Ability is a "must-have" attribute for any potential protégé. The motivation aspect of the formula is shared between the mentor and the protégé, because it is always a mix of external and internal motivation that drives anyone. The support aspect belongs to the mentor. When all three of these things are in play, success is the only result.

- Your starting point has to be one of loving people, being wise, caring, and compassionate.
- The competencies required by the mentor, in order to be successful, are centered on compatibility.
- The protégé is taking in influences from all around him, and he emulates little pieces of all those influencers to create his own style. Our job as mentors is not so much about style as it is substance.
- Both parties in the relationship need to hold each other accountable for the success or failure of the task. Dialogue needs to occur when one party feels slighted, or feels that the other party isn't listening, or more likely, doesn't understand exactly what the other is trying to communicate.
- High potential protégés are expected to deliver results, be inspiring leaders, think critically, be flexible, innovative,

collaborative AND be able to lead influentially.

- Performance = ability x motivation x support.

Exercises

- Think about being a high potential protégé, with all of the skill sets and competencies that are needed for the job. Sounds stressful, right? Now, if you are the protégé, what can your mentor do for you to make that load easier? If you are the mentor, what can you do for your protégé to make his or her job less overwhelming? Come up with a list.

- Think about the formula mentioned near the end of the chapter. Performance = ability x motivation x support. In your current job, what, if any of these factors are lacking, thereby preventing you from doing your best work possible? How might someone be able to supply the missing factors?

Chapter Twelve:

Can Your Organization Benefit? And How?

Many organizations today are setting up mentoring and coaching programs. They're setting these up for very good, smart reasons—these programs are backed up by research and proven effectiveness, and they're a good change from how businesses have operated in the past. Years ago, I worked for a man who should have never been promoted into a leadership role, and he did not handle the task very well when he was. He was a perfect example of The Peter Principle. For those not old enough to know, The Peter Principle is a concept in management theory in which the selection of a candidate for a position is based on the candidate's performance in their current role, rather than on abilities relevant to the intended role. Thus, employees only stop being promoted once they can no longer perform effectively, and "managers rise to the level of their incompetence." The principle is named after Laurence J. Peter, who co-authored, with Raymond Hull, the humorous 1969 book, *The Peter Principle: Why Things Always Go Wrong.*

Needless to say, the example I'm telling you about was incompetent in his dealings with his subordinates, so the senior management team decided to get him some help—let's say training. This gentleman told us they were sending him to "charm school." Now, the way it worked in the 80s was they sent him to a workplace psychologist, who ran him through a series of tests to figure out why he had no leadership capability and why no one on his staff was interested in working with him or supporting him. See, he had been promoted to his level of incompetence. His training or lack of training made him ineffective as a leader. It also made him ineffective as a manager. We could train him to become a decent manager, but we could not instill the leadership skills in him to make him effective.

Thank God we are living in today's world, where charm school no longer exists; now we have coaches who help people like our ineffective leader/manager improve and work on their specific issues. Coaching and mentoring programs exist in just about every major organization today because executives are concerned about performance, workplace violence, liability issues, and sexual harassment lawsuits, and really work to prevent things from going wrong. In addition to that, coaching and mentoring programs are a recruitment tool as well. If your organization does not have a specific program, I would ask your human resource representative why they don't. It can only enhance your organizational effectiveness.

There are some other very strong reasons for mentoring and coaching programs. Bonnie Hagemann and Saundra Stroope, in "Bringing Your A-Game," mention that, "According to a study by the Vaya Group, 40% of high potential job moves end in failure, and up to 64% of high potentials say that development assignments are having little impact on their development," (18). This echoes what Michael Arklind writes in "Leaders of Tomorrow":

> This shows that there is a strong need for individual coaches and mentors. Regardless of whether you are work for a manufacturer, distributor, consultancy, or technology firm, your staying power and ongoing success in the future will ultimately

> be determined by one single factor, your future leaders. (10)

The research also points to other reasons for implementing these kinds of programs. Phillip Perry, citing Linda Phillips-Jones, writes, “Capturing knowledge in the workplace is especially critical today, given the nation's demographic shift…Thousands of baby boomers are about to retire. By having mentoring in place your more skilled people can pass on their knowledge in a structured way," (46). So it’s about passing on what amounts to the DNA of a company, but it’s also about more than that. It’s also about change. As I have stressed before, if our companies are not leading the pack, they are falling behind. Shirley Chan agrees with me, writing:

> To have a competitive advantage, it is important to attract staff who possess skills and competencies to work effectively in a business environment that includes sudden economic expansions and contractions, diverse cultural influences, and fast-paced

> technological changes that involve workplace communications as well as new services and products. Training and mentoring programs should reflect such changes in the business environment. (23)

If we don't have the ability to adjust when problems arise, we become cultural dinosaurs. Imagine yourself in 1994, right at the advent of the Internet Era. Now imagine that your boss has just doubled your company's investment in typewriters. Would you feel confident in your corporation?

Companies need younger workers to supply new vision, but younger workers often need direction. This is why mentoring programs are oftentimes the best of both worlds, as they give the company the benefit of a younger mindset and they give younger workers more fulfillment and the benefit of experience. Max Messmer brings up this same point, writing:

> Mentors can foster teamwork and improve staff motivation, and—by sharing their

> expertise—can also increase employee competency levels.
>
> At the same time, mentors enhance their value to the organization. Serving as advisors allows them to build supervisory, leadership, and training abilities—skills that are valuable for any accountant. In addition, being asked to serve in this capacity shows the company respects their work, which can lead to higher job satisfaction and retention. (17)

This all leads back to the value of mentoring programs, both on a personal and a professional scale. Every party involved has something to gain from this kind of arrangement.

I imagine you might be thinking of the bottom line right now. "This mentoring program stuff sounds expensive." Depending on the commitment you put into it, it may be. But what's more expensive, continually hiring people who come into your company only to leave for what they perceive as greener pastures, or hiring people who stay in your company because they are satisfied and feel valued? If that sounds like a no-brainer, it's because it is. Stephen Morel says it even better than I can. He writes:

> The rewards and benefits to your employees will outweigh the cost of implementation. First, employees that are successfully oriented to your organization's culture and the work that will be done are productive sooner than those who struggle to acclimate. Second, lower turnover equals cost savings by reducing replacement hiring and recruitment advertising need. (no page number)

David Rock and Ruth Donde, in "Driving organizational change with internal coaching programs," say it another way:

> Some research says that 35 percent of new executives failed within the first eighteen months of starting a new position in 2004. The huge cost involved in finding people, training them and then having to do that all over again, makes it a worthwhile

> investment to reduce that number dramatically. (15)

Why did these new hires fail? I'd hazard a guess that their companies did not have adequate programs in place to help them adjust to their new workspace. Mentoring programs are one of the best and surest investments your organization can make.

Now that I have made my case for mentoring programs, the question naturally arises, "When do I implement a program like this?" The answer is, "During the onboarding process." Morel, citing David Lee, writes that onboarding is "…the process of integrating new employees into an organization; preparing them to succeed at their job and become fully engaged, productive members of the organization," (no page number). Rock and Donde describe onboarding as being "…about bringing people from the outside into the business. It can be cross-organization, e.g. someone joining a whole new team and a whole new function; it can also be expatriates moving to the same organization in another country," (15). Even if the employee in question has worked at the company for fifteen years and is simply switching departments, there might be elements of estrangement and discomfort that a mentoring program can nip in the bud. Almost everyone can benefit from a mentoring program that treats new employees with respect and doesn't take old employees for granted. Onboarding is clearly the most effective time to engage with new employees and set them up with coaches or mentors.

Mentors are the backbone of any program implemented during the onboarding process, and their importance cannot be understated. Morel writes, "The mentor or 'partner' is responsible for making sure the new hire is acclimated quickly by being designated as the 'go-to' person for questions about day-to-day activities, tasks or the company in general. A mentor provides a safe environment for those answers," (no page number). All of this responsibility falls on the mentor, but as a man or woman with experience, the mentor is ready for it.

As I've already mentioned, however, sometimes successful mentoring comes down to compatibility. Not every mentor will be right for every protégé. Dan Steer, in "ONBOARD With It All," reminds us that there are certain questions we need to mull over when deciding how best to implement our program. He writes:

> When you consider whom to involve in onboarding, ask yourself:
>
> • With whom will each new hire work?
>
> • Which formal and informal networks will affect the new hires' success?
>
> • Who are the subject matter experts who can best help new hires get up to speed?
>
> • Who will coach or mentor each new starter?
>
> • When and how will management get involved? (29)

When humans are involved no process will ever be perfect, but with foresight and some deep thought, we can dramatically increase our workers' productivity and satisfaction.

How do you measure effectiveness?

So now that you've decided for your organization or yourself to effectively mentor, just how do you quantify results and measure your effectiveness? Kira Fickenscher, in "How to effectively measure mentoring programs," tells us how to do just that. She says that we should start:

- **Improving managerial competency** with competency-based mentoring for managers at various levels.
- **Improving leadership bench strength** through identification of high-potential employees to cultivate leadership skills, including relationship development with an executive sponsor.

- **Improving time to proficiency for new hires** by a mandatory six-month mentoring program for new skill and role training.

- **Retaining and transferring knowledge** through situational and topical mentoring around high-value, tacit knowledge areas.

- **Creating an inclusive, diverse culture** with individual sponsorship, dedicated special interest groups and career development support.

- **Retaining talent through a long-term** career planning and personal development mentoring program.

These principles are particularly significant if you are running a mentoring program for your organization. However, even if you are doing these on a personal basis, it is very important for you to figure out what progress you might be making with your protégé.

Just as in any business process, developing a set of Key Performance Indicators and making them part of the processes or people you are measuring is key to the success of your company's mentoring program. On a personal level, in most cases the measurements are far more abstract, but important nonetheless.

In her article, Fickenscher tells us that there are effective ways to structure KPIs as well:

- If our objective is to retain talent, we can measure this through retention rates, employee engagement, and employee satisfaction.

- To create an inclusive and diverse culture, track advancement rates, retention rates, and the employee perception of an organization.

- If our goal is improve managerial competency, we should evaluate expertise based on competency assessment, the number of sessions completed on average per mentored employee, internal promotions within the ranks, improved job performance ratings, and the achievement of individual development targets.

When we follow these principles, we are putting ourselves on our best footing possible to make a success of the partnership. Nothing involving people and interpersonal relationships can be guaranteed, but implemented properly, these guidelines will ensure a quantifiable rise in job performance and satisfaction.

Takeaways

- If our companies are not innovating, they are falling behind.

- Mentoring and coaching programs have to incorporate change and adaptation into their design in order to keep up with the challenges of the modern world.

- Mentors are the backbone of any program implemented during the onboarding process, and their importance cannot be understated.

- Developing a set of Key Performance Indicators and making them part of the processes or people you are measuring is key to the success of your company's mentoring program.

- Say you're mentoring a new employee as part of the onboarding process. What are some of the strategies you can use to retain him or her, without sounding like a corporate mouthpiece or giving them false promises? Is money always the answer to retention, or are there other factors at play? Name some of the factors, if you can think of any, and work on finding ways to implement them.

- What do you think are some elements that are important when developing a set of Key Performance Indicators. What traits are important to leadership, important to the employees, and important to both parties combined? What kind of investment has to go into each element to make the onboarding process successful?

Chapter Thirteen:

Robust Business Relationships

I have learned over my thirty-plus years in business that the main things that make a business relationship prosper and survive are always centered on trust. I hate to use this phrase, because sometimes it is overused and rendered meaningless, but the phrase "win-win" is key in all business relationships. What we mean by win-win is that both parties are successful in getting what they want out of the relationship. It means that there is no unfair advantage and one party doesn't feel like it is being played by the other in and taken advantage of in that particular situation. To a certain extent this win-win idea has been played down by many executives who consider relationships to be only in their favor and don't believe that strong relationships, if played right, can get you just about anything you want in business success.

It reminds me of a partnership a supplier had with their customer in an automotive plant. They told me that they were penalized for every minute the production line went down—and it went down at a pretty astronomical rate. While I was in their plant, their own production line was stalled because the automotive plants line was down due to a major forecasting issue. Now, I knew the answer to this question before I asked it, but I asked anyway, "So this partnership you have with this automotive supplier causes you to pay for their downtime when you've caused an issue with their production, right? So, when they cause a line stoppage for you, they pay you for your downtime, correct?" They laughed and said, "You know it doesn't work that way..." This made me ask, "Why doesn't it work that way? It is a partnership, correct?" The supplier ended up locating its feeder facility right on the same property as the automotive plant. Even though, I really believe there is a deeper issue here. A solution that penalized one party and not the other would have been a wiser choice. I would have tried to negotiate a more fair and equitable solution that made both parties whole.

I will give you another example: I always believed I had a knack for creating partnerships, and I would negotiate many intangibles with suppliers (stuff that could not be measured as effectively as need be). I mean things like ESI, (Early Supplier Involvement), VMI (Vendor Managed Inventory), DFM/DFA (Design for Manufacturability and Design for Assembly), and Joint Cost Reduction Teams (cost reduction isn't only the supplier's issue, as it has a lot to do with how the customer forecasts, plans, releases orders, stores material, etc... These are proven techniques to drive excess costs out of the equation. Our customers had no programs like this, and we were leading the pack. One day a VP and General Manager said we needed immediate cost reductions, and they asked me to send a letter to the supply base asking for a 10% rollback on prices, and if we did not get it, we would send all of the material we bought from them out to bid on the open market.

Now, were we a distressed business? Were we under tremendous pressure from the board to enhance profitability? Were we trying to take market share away from a competitor? Were we meeting a challenge from a customer who had these issues? The answer to all of the above was

“NO.” The answer I got from this executive was an unbelievable, “Our customers do it to us, so why don’t we do it to our suppliers?” This was reactionary management, not proactive management. Why was it that we could take the time and react to a customer, but we couldn’t tell our customers, here is how we continuously reduce your costs and give you a much better solution, by taking all of the waste out of the system, through ESI, DFM, kaizen, kanbans, etc…? You see, that relational approach takes time, professionalism and a proactive philosophy of business that we have lost over time, having become more or less reactionary. This is why partnerships are so difficult to achieve.

Now, think about this: if organizations can’t achieve those partnering relationships because of all the bias in the relationship, how difficult must it be for individuals to achieve this high level or understanding? Isn’t it human nature to “go for the jugular,” and just “get what you deserve”? But how does that fly in the face of mentoring and coaching and a relationship that is built on trust, commitment, respect, and a shared vision? I don't mention these stories to suggest it is impossible to build the kind of effective business relationships you want, but I do it because I want you to fully understand how organizations and simple human nature work against these kinds of relationships all the time.

I keep on coming back to these cardinal points, but that's because they're so important. I think that in developing a successful and strong business relationship, we must always consider the following:

> **Trust.** This is tough stuff for corporate America to buy. They trust no one. I think it is hard to develop a trusting relationship with business partners when we are focused on our own individual organization's goals, and we put the partner's goals as secondary. It is a unique organization that can develop trust with its suppliers or customers and that will make this work. That makes it even tougher for

the individuals that work in these organizations to develop trust themselves. By the same token, it is a unique individual who has the confidence to step up and make a difference and understand that "trust" is the basis of all relationships.

Respect for one another's position. Always remember that everyone works for someone. You can't always be in a position to win, and compromise is the safest and sometimes best way out. Look for a way of achieving that sought after "win-win" goal. It is tough, I know that, and the relationship will be tested many times, so think of your alternatives and have a game plan. This is something that should not be thought of lightly. True cooperation and understanding with compassion for the other party is difficult and not very prevalent in our damage mitigating society. But the first step is the ability to listen and understand.

Honesty. I really believe honesty is understated whenever we talk about it. All of us have flaws, and none of us are perfect, so why are we trying to pretend that we are? Dishonesty breeds distrust, because people—unless they were born yesterday—can tell when someone else is trying to take advantage of them. So cut out that problem entirely by not pretending we are better, and just being honest about our shortcomings. So let's get out in the open and stop looking for ways to hide our imperfections. Speaking of which…

Imperfections. Let's look for ways to embrace those and help each other succeed. But to do that, it takes commitment and compassion. As I was writing this, a country music superstar had passed. Little Jimmy Dickens was ninety-four, and he was the longest active member of The Grand Ole Opry. Little Jimmy was known for his short stature and big heart. I happened to look up an interview he did for

West Virginia Public Television about seven years ago. The host asked him what he wanted to be known or remembered for. His answer? "Honesty." I sat back and thought of that; here was a man who had a seventy-year singing and performing career, who did not want to be remembered for his work, but for his work ethic. This goes back to the earlier chapter on character. Honesty defines one's character.

Living up to one's commitments. I really struggle with this. This one defies human nature and the competitive spirit. Yes, I know that a true partnership needs this, but when it comes to crunch time we always protect ourselves, and that is wrong in a personal sense. In a business sense, I have seen very few times where the partnership doesn't fall apart over living, or not living, up to one's commitments. If it's your fault, take the blame and do everything you can to fix the problem. If you own up to what's happened and you do it in a positive way, only good things will come from it. People will know that you care enough about the partnership to sacrifice your ego for it, and that will in turn inspire them to push harder. We try to protect ourselves because we don't want to be humiliated, but there are much larger things at stake in a business environment than our own problems. The sooner we understand that, the better.

Eliminating the surprises. There is nothing worse in business. If we could eliminate all the surprises we would be far more efficient, but new ones lurk at every corner. If we could find a way to control them, our business relationships would be much smoother, but there seems to always be some higher level executive trying to exert their "power" into the equation. That does far more harm than good in most cases. The best thing to do is factor them into the plans beforehand. Plan for the worst and hope for the best, but do be prepared. You may not know what will come at you in the course of your project, but you do know that something will pop up, and when it does, you will have factored in time, personnel issues, budgets, and other concerns in order to handle the surprise successfully.

Looking at clients as more than a revenue stream. That is why I always say personal relationships come before business relationships, in almost all cases, and sometimes the business relationship is the most difficult one to have, even though it seems like it would be the easier of the two. Are you willing to walk away because it isn't the right fit? If you aren't, you are looking at the relationship from a revenue stream only, and it typically will not last. If you are looking solely at the bottom line, ask yourself if you are the kind of partner that someone would want to have. Sometimes change starts from within; just because we find out we have contributed to a problem scenario in the past doesn't mean we can't be productive in the future. Life, just like business, is about growth, and there is always room for us to improve and build healthier relationships.

Sharing or having a vision of partnership. The term 'partnership" is way overused in the business world, and oftentimes it is said to be a partnership when it is good for me and takes advantage of you. Be careful of using this word, because in true partnerships, parties have a vested interest in one another. It really doesn't need to be monetary, but most often it is to make the "partnership" effective. I've just asked you to ask yourself if you're the kind of partner you'd wish to have. Now I'm asking you to think about the kinds of partners you have and the kind that you want. If you aren't in a good situation, what can you do to improve it? Look at your potential partners and protégés carefully.

Can you find a mentoring relationship within a business relationship environment? I believe you can, but there are some caveats. Remember, if mentoring is about one's personal transformation, all outside influences are valued. Sometimes the business relationship gets in the way of effective mentoring, and you need to be careful of this. As I stated before, business relationships last as long as both sides are receiving what they need from the relationship. When one side sees no value, typically the relationship will end, whether both sides want that or not. I still do believe that mentoring can happen in a business relationship, though, if you are perceptive enough to grasp it. Years ago I met an older gentleman (about twenty-five years my senior) who ran a small company out of Indianapolis. Even though I was a seasoned executive of forty, I learned quite a bit from John. John was a polished senior executive who shared many stories, which, once I absorbed and understood them, made me a far better leader than any leadership program I could have attended.

John was a successful entrepreneur who told me that sometimes his reps (manufacturers' representatives) made more money in a year than he did. Think about it—here was an entrepreneur and eventually a business owner who was paying the rep group more than he was making. Why, you might ask? He valued the relationship with the rep. Yes, he was the one who had to worry constantly about cash flow, reinvestment in the business, sales forecasts, employee issues, market penetration, and all of the things a business owner lies awake at night thinking about. But remember, he had made a commitment, and like we spoke of earlier, life is based on character and integrity, and he was not going back on his word. Eventually his business grew, and through the help of his reps, he didn't have to worry about that situation again, because he took care of them and they took care of him. That is the way life works when you build a life of character and integrity. It is where I learned the most about character and integrity, and I bet that he didn't even realize that he was teaching it.

See, the best teachers are the ones who don't realize they are teaching us. They teach us through their actions and words, not in a classroom. Think about that, and think about what business relationships have taught you, and how they are not just useful in your business life, but in your personal life as well. Now, I can tell you many stories of John like that, but you get the point.

John taught me to make anything, whether it was dinner, lunch, or just a cup of coffee, into an event. He taught me how to engage the waitress, waiter, or restaurant owner in conversation, which led to superior service and eventually into another relationship that could be fostered. I remember taking him to a great little Italian restaurant in my home town, and he always ordered the veal chop. I remember him telling the owner that it was the best veal chop between New York and Chicago, which made the owner glow with pride. Now, I am sure it was a damn good veal chop, but did it classify as “the best”? Who knows, but it did guarantee us a great meal and superior service, and the owners always looked forward to us returning. Not only did he leave the host a nice tip, he left them with a sense of pride and accomplishment for having served us. Cool. It makes me wonder today what his employees felt about him, and just how much compassion he had for the folks that worked for him. See, to John, this was genuine. This was not a show—it was who he was.

John taught me that you always grab the check and you never let anyone else pay for dinner—I learned that it's a small token to pay for loyalty and building the relationship. Even today, I tell friends who say they want to pick up the tab that they have to negotiate that in advance with me, because I automatically pick up the check. I could tell you many a story about John, but the main point is that we had a strong business relationship based on trust, and he taught me so much about how to be polished, professional, and known for your trusting character. John is retired today and living in Florida, so whenever I go to Florida for spring training, time willing, I try to see him and his wife, and he still beats me at grabbing the check.

It is what we learn and glean from others that are important in establishing just who we are as a person, boss, or leader. So next time you are in a social setting, pick up on the little things that you notice and ask yourself why people do what they do. Think back on John and how he led by example…how he created a learning environment when there was not learning environment established. We were not in school, yet we were being schooled. Isn't it better to be educated in the way things should be done and why they should be done that way?

So there are ways to turn a business relationship into a mentoring experience for the protégé, but just like the old saying goes, "The teacher will appear when the student is ready to learn." You have to be open and recognize opportunities to learn from great teachers as well, even when they don’t realize they are teaching.

Takeaways

- Both parties being successful in getting what they want out of the relationship is key to a productive business relationship.

- We need to keep coming back to the cardinal points that are the basis of human relationships if we hope for ours to be successful.

- Business relationships only last as long as both sides are receiving what they need from the relationship.

- Be like John in my story; teach while no one realizes they are being taught.

- Keep in mind that, "When the student is ready to learn, the teacher will appear."

- If you are in a business relationship that is working for you, but the other party does not feel that he is "winning," is there anything you can do to prevent the relationship from collapsing? Think about what you might ask him to find out what is really bothering him. Think about the cost to you to ensure his happiness, and weigh that against what the partnership is worth. Develop a plan regarding this.

- Say you are looking for a mentor, but your company doesn't have a mentoring program in place. What are some steps you can take to make your desire known? Think about who you might be able to talk to, whether in company or outside. Who do you admire and respect, either business wise or personally, and do these qualities intersect in your potential mentor? Draw up a list of traits you need in a mentor, and then ask yourself who might match them.

Chapter Fourteen:

Next Steps

When do I really need help? How do I become a mentor and make a difference?

In conclusion, what can we say about mentoring? Go back to The Mentor Matrix as a quick reference on when you might utilize the various strategies talked about in this book. Use the various concepts and examples as a way of helping you figure out the best approach for you or your organization. Hopefully, the stories I have told you about in this book really help to make you visualize these situations. Think of your legacy and what you will leave on this earth. How will you make it better for future generations? What is your contribution? What will lead to your fulfillment? And of course, how does all of that help other people and make a difference in their lives?

Remember, when we started this journey, I told you I am no expert in mentoring and coaching. Everything I learned about the process was done by trial and error, but lo and behold, the folks I interacted with have said, "You really have a knack for this, you really know how to engage and guide others as well as listen to what they are really saying, and it has served you well over the years." Remember the racquetball story that started this book off? Trial, error, experimentation...yeah, you got it. So many people ask, "Can you teach us to do it?" Well, this book was an attempt to do such a thing. It was an attempt to take what seems to me to be a relatively simple thing and make sure more of us can do it, and do it effectively.

So go back and look at your skills, either personally, professionally, or organizationally, and look at where you fail. Really give them an honest assessment. Are you unhappy? Are your employees unhappy? Are they all unproductive because they lack direction or attention? Do a quick survey of these attributes. The survey should consist of the following:

> **Would I describe my organization as a learning organization?** By that I mean, do my people have the basic skills to think on their own? Would they flourish in an

environment where they could manage some of their own initiatives? What happens when you give them projects? Do they flourish or flounder? This is the first step to empowering your team, because you want them to be successful right off the bat. They cannot fail at this. If they aren't a learning organization, create an environment where you make it fun to work as part of a team, to try new things, and grow together.

Create a specific exercise as part of the onboarding process that addresses these issues, and create regular opportunities for both new and experienced employees that measure changes. This exercise should take place in a low-pressure situation, where the overall outcome is one of bonding and teamwork rather than stress. Small opportunities to learn can lead to big results down the road.

Pick the leaders. Out of that first exercise, you will quickly see who the leaders are and who the followers are. You will be able to judge individuals' potentials for leading and start to give them deeper assignments. Give them the opportunity to lead. Keep in mind that some may be vocal leaders and some may only lead by their example. Both styles of leaders are important to have within your organization. Both types of leaders can help transform your organization.

Give your potential leaders specific tasks and the freedom to do those tasks, and when the job is done, give them feedback on what they did well and what they need to work on. Always start with what they did well. Tactfulness is vital. When giving someone feedback, it is important to remember to start off on a positive tone, as this makes the constructive criticism much easier to take and absorb.

Get the leaders focused on the task. Be it an improvement project, a cultural shift, getting the organization focused, increasing the sales team's efforts, or whatever else it might be, it is always important to sit down with your leadership team and put in writing what they are trying to accomplish. If you are trying to get the inside sales team to improve the closure rate of calls, focus on exactly how the leaders are going to help the team do that. This becomes a coaching opportunity, and you will not know how dynamic this can be until you try it. If done correctly, you will see the empowerment before your eyes. If you skip some of the steps, be prepared for failure. Every plan needs a course of action, and this is your time to make that course of action. Remember to plan for contingencies. General Patton and General Pershing did not send their troops into battle without a well thought-out plan. If they had forgotten those intricate steps, we would be speaking German or Russian today.

Put the measurement system in place. This is key. What is your measure of success? How do you know if you are making progress or regressing? As the ultimate leader of your organization, you need to keep your finger on the pulse of your organization's improvement by monitoring where your team members are at in real time. The reason for doing this is simple. It is much easier to correct or fix problems while they are happening, rather than once they are complete and are catastrophic. Once things have solidified, they are much harder to change—don't let problems get to that point.

I have done a lot of industrial engineering work, and we teach this philosophy called synchronous flow of materials. We believe in doing one part at a time through the flow. Doing one part at a time through the flow means we can catch any quality issue with the component and not build a whole bunch of scrap. This is part of our zero waste mentality. Apply that to your team with mistakes or wrong deployment efforts. Catch it quickly and your costs will be minimized as well.

Reward the team. Rewards help build the continuum of success. Take the team to dinner, make an associate of the month, give them praise in front of the team. I helped an engine manufacturer transform their facility one time and they gave me the "Catalyst Award." What is a catalyst, you might ask? I think it is the very key in business transformations. The dictionary says a catalyst is "a substance that increases the rate of a chemical reaction without itself undergoing any permanent chemical change." In other words, the person who has contributed the most for change in a business.

Why don't you create your own award and do something special for your people? Teach your people that you value innovation and creativity, and this will inspire them to give you more potentially groundbreaking ideas. Bring in pizza, take them to dinner, and take them to dinner with their spouses. I'm not talking about huge rewards here—people appreciate little gestures, however easy or inexpensive, because these let them know that they are important to you. These steps go a long way toward building a team. Be a catalyst.

All of these things need to happen in an organization before it can really be effective with a mentoring program. Starting a mentoring program within your organization is the easy part, making it effective and establishing a fertile ground for mentoring to work is far more difficult. The mistake most organizations make today when deciding to put in "official" mentoring programs is that the ground needs to be plowed over first. You need to create the right environment for people to grow. Therefore you need to go back to trust, integrity, and character. Remember those words, because they have to be in place personally as well as professionally for mentoring to work.

Why is all of this important to business today? There is one simple answer…human capital. See, we can have the latest equipment, the best IT systems, and the fanciest offices, but if we don't have people to run them and work them and make them successful, we will fail. Many of us, who focus on business improvement, realize that we need capital to make things work. We not only need money, which we will call working capital, but we need intellectual capital—technological capital as well as human capital. In 2015, people still make all of the other capital needs work.

Why am I bringing this up? Because we spend far less money on investment in human capital than we do in all of the other capital needs. Take out labor costs from human capital, which I would argue is not human capital, and we spend far less. But we should be spending far more, and here is why…mentoring, coaching, and developing robust business relationships should be part of your human capital strategy. We said earlier in the book that millennials expect to be mentored and have support programs, and all of the other generations that work in our businesses agree it is a nice to have these benefits and it is the right thing to do.

When people are more engaged with the business goals and the intricacies of the business, they are more likely to do what is best for them and their continuing role within that business. In 2007, I did a huge turnaround of a plant in the Midwest for a company you would all be too familiar with. This was an operation that had had success as a muffler plant, but the parent decided it was going to make it an integrated assembly operation. That was the key to the long term survival of this relatively small operation. It made this operation more sophisticated and complex from a manufacturing standpoint. The parent invested in a state-of-the-art assembly line, but they forgot a couple of major concerns. First, the people at this plant did not know how to make a complex part because they were used to welding rather low tech mufflers. Secondly, the leadership did not realize that the skill set of the management team needed to be a little different for this operation. Luckily, we got there just in time to save it, and we actually increased employment five-fold. For as great as the mother ship was, they lost sight of one particular thing.

State-of-the-art equipment can't be run by the folks who run the welding operation without the proper training and leadership. That means people. That means mentoring programs. That means having a plan and matching the right mentors with the right protégés. That is where they failed, but they were lucky. Without a mentoring program and the foresight to run it, how lucky will other businesses be?

We did some rather simple things to turn this company around, and one of the key things was getting the folks on the shop floor engaged. That was the easiest part. Many times I have to remind clients that we are not building a rocket. People are a key part of the equation. The best way to the solution, as simple as this may sound, is to talk to the folks who do it every day for a living. Now they can't always tell you what is wrong, but they can tell you how they do their job. When you hear their stories, you can quickly figure out just what is going wrong. This all goes along with aligning goals up and down the organization.

This same organization sent me to one of their plants to fix an accounting process issue. Now, without getting into the specifics, let's just say it was an easy process to fix. It seemed as if they were going to miss their bonuses just because of this simple (so we thought at the time) process issue. Went I got to the plant, the first thing I did was sit down with the process owner and ask her if she had ever mapped her process. Of course she hadn't, and we proceeded to do that. I showed her the waste in the process and got her to buy in to try it my way. She bought into it and the process was fixed in a matter of days. There was one fly in the ointment, however; we had fixed the process there, but just like anything else, it is a chain of processes that makes this work or fail.

I called our sponsor and he congratulated me on fixing the issue. I remember it clearly, as if it were yesterday, when I explained to him the old snake eating the squirrel story. By fixing the process there, we just moved the bottleneck to another operation and they would have to deal with it at the next point. I told him that in order to have a systemic fix; we needed to address the problem holistically. We needed to look at all of the connectivity points and fix the entire chain. He bought into that, and in six weeks we had the problem fixed. The most rewarding part of that story, however, is the fact that the process owner I had dealt with at the beginning thanked me profusely. She told me, "See, they thought it was me, that I was the problem. They never realized that with a little guidance and coaching and understanding of just what was important, I could fix it." That was a beautiful day as a consultant and as a mentor, to know we had made systemic change, and that the folks that were involved appreciated the change they had been through. The client was ecstatic, and they learned a little something that day. They learned that by a little process mapping and guidance we can fix just about any problem they can throw at us. This example also goes along with aligning goals up and down the organization. When people feel valued and realize that the individual contributes to the whole, the organization can function smoothly, as it is supposed to run. In an organization, everything is connected, and the sooner we realize that, the sooner we can start working for the team.

- How will you make it better for future generations? What is your contribution? What will lead to your fulfillment? And how does all of that help other people and make a difference in their lives?
- Trial, error, experimentation—these are all important to your specific mentoring process.
- Look at your skills, either personally, professionally, or organizationally, and look at where you fail.
- Some leaders are vocal and some may only lead by their example. Both styles of leaders are important to have within your organization.
- Use the mentoring program you have in place to help align goals up and down the organization.

Exercises

- It's time to be honest with yourself. Where do you fail? Draw up a list of your traits—which ones you think are admirable, which ones you think you need to work on. Don't beat yourself up over the bad ones; instead, make a few practical notes next to each flaw, notes that show ways you can turn these traits around. Remember, keep the goals attainable, and work on the smaller ones first to give you the boost of instant gratification.
- Do you think of yourself as a leader? Using the list that you just made, apply the different styles of leadership to it, and find out just what kind of leader you are. If you don't think that you have any leadership skills, ask yourself what you can work on to develop these.

Chapter Fifteen:

What legacy will you leave?

While I was finishing up this book, I read an obituary about a baseball player, Dave Bergman, who had just passed way too early age of 61. This is what was in *The Detroit News* soon after his death:

> *Detroit — Dave Bergman, the left-handed-hitting first baseman whose acquisition in spring training 1984 was a pivotal move for a Tigers team that would go on to win the World Series, passed away Monday, the Tigers confirmed.*
>
> *He was 61, and had been in a long fight with bile-duct cancer, the same disease that Ernie Harwell battled.*
>
> *"Dave was as spirited a person as he was a player," the Tigers said in a statement. "He will forever hold a special place in Tigers history for the versatile roles he played, and his significant contributions as a member of the 1984 world champion Tigers. We will miss seeing Bergie at the ballpark and in the community."*

He was a smooth-fielding first baseman — he was one of the best at the old hidden-ball trick, with Alan Wiggins of the Orioles and Ozzie Guillen of the White Sox his two famous victims — and carried a reputation as a great teammate, on and off the field. He also was a longtime union rep.

"Bergie, going back to my rookie year (1987), he took me under his wing," said Mike Henneman, a teammate of Bergman's from 1987-92. "He was just a 100-percent class man, in every aspect of life. A huge loss."

Bergman last was at Comerica Park this past summer as part of the 1984 World Series reunion. While he wore his trademark smile, it was clear the illness was taking its toll, as he'd lost so much weight and hair. While battling the illness, though, Bergman always chose not to discuss his health.

Asked again at the World Series reunion, he smiled but declined again so not to take attention away from the 1984 team. During the pregame ceremony June 30 at Comerica Park, Bergman put on a glove and played first base while Alan Trammell and Lou Whitaker turned one more double play.

"Dave served as a beloved mentor to me, a patient sounding board, a brave coach and a wise counselor," said Robert Bilkie, Bergman's longtime business partner. "He inspired me with his humility and decency. I believe that the true measure of a man is the cumulative success that he breeds in others. In this regard, Dave truly belongs in the Humanity Hall of Fame."

Jeff Daniels tweeted, "Saddened to hear about the loss of Dave Bergman. A great friend who took his success and used it time and again to give back to others."

The reason this struck me as I was writing is simple. Unless you were a significant baseball fan or a Tigers fan, you may not have known Bergman's story, but there is a lot there. Caring, sharing, mentoring, humility....and well, we won't live forever. Life is about one's mark on the earth, on another individual, or on another family. There are thousands of Dave Bergmans who will never get their due or great credit, but who make the world go around because they understand just what their actions do to others.

I mentioned my mentors early on in this book. You won't find their names in the history books, and long after I am gone their effects will be marginalized, but they have had a tremendous impact on me, and through them I have had a tremendous impact on others. So in a sense, I guess they live on through the chain of lives they have affected. I will say this again, although by now you should understand that very few of the people you've touched will tell you about how you touched them—but never underestimate your scope in just how many people you are actually influencing. It is far greater than you know.

Empower yourself through mentoring, coaching, or creating a significant business relationship. Become someone's friend and help them through trying times, and you will be rewarded many times over—that is what the mentoring story is about. It is about how you leave your mark on this earth; it is about how the world is better off because you were here; it is about being a farmer who cultivates what he grows; and most importantly, it is about fulfillment—your fulfillment. You see, how many times have we said this world is not about us, but about others? That is what mentoring does for you and others. Do it because it makes you happy to give back. Hopefully, you live long enough so that material goods are not important, and you can watch the joy on people's faces as you give it all away.

I know it's corny, but living your life as it were your last day is probably the way we all should live. Shouldn't we continually question ourselves as to what legacy we are leaving on this earth? Who have I touched today, and just how is this world a better place because I had an influence on it? These are important questions when it comes to mentoring, coaching, and developing stronger and more significant business relationships. These may sound just like words on a page, but take them to heart, and commit to changing the world in your own way. Understand your gifts, and understand the rewards, as these will lead to a very fulfilling life.

Mentoring, coaching (to a somewhat lesser extent), and developing strong business relationships (to an even lesser extent), lead to a very fulfilling and rewarding life, but all of these concepts and principles that you learn—with all of their integral concepts—can lead to a very enriching life for you. In many cases, it is difficult to understand the mark you leave on people, and you often don't discover that mark until later in life, or unless on the rare occurrence someone tells you.

Fulfillment as a noun means satisfaction or happiness as a result of fully developing one's abilities or character. I think, as part of that fulfillment model, we are all seeking mentoring and coaching in our lives, and our relationships with others play a huge role in determining our happiness. So become fulfilled. Become happy. Show others that you care. Live your life to the fullest, and share your ambitions, dreams, and experiences with others. Make a difference through mentoring someone, coaching them to success, or just by enriching them through a relationship. You will be glad you did. It will reward you many times.

Takeaways

- Life is about one's mark on the earth, on another individual, or on another family.

- Never underestimate your scope in just how many people you are actually influencing.

- It is about how you leave your mark on this earth; it is about how the world is better off because you were here; it is about being a farmer who cultivates what he grows; and most importantly, it is about fulfillment—your fulfillment.

- Our relationships with others play a huge role in determining our happiness.

- If you aren't making your mark on people right now, how can you change that? List three doable, practical ways that you can start improving your life and others', and implement them

- Ask yourself if your relationships with others are where they should be. If they aren't, what can you do to improve them? Ask yourself if any of these non-optimal relationships could potentially be profitable. Which ones can be salvaged, and which ones are too far gone? What would be the benefits to salvaging the relationships?

Sources

Arklind, Michael. “Leaders of Tomorrow.” *Smart Business Northern California.* (May 2014).

Baylor University’s Mentoring for Adolescent Development. “Stages of a Mentoring Relationship.” *Mentoring.org.*

Beck, Michael. "Core Competencies." *Leadership Excellence* 28, no. 3 (March 2011): 6.

Berfield, Susan. “Mentoring can be Messy.” *Businessweek* no. 4019 (January 29, 2007): 80-81.

Bloomberg, Mark. "The Role of Mentoring." *Physician Executive* 40, no. 2 (March, 2014): 88-90.

Chan, Shirley. "People Management in the Context of Global Change." *Employment Relations Today (Wiley)* 29, no. 2 (Summer, 2002): 19-24.

Cohen, Allan R., and David L. Bradford. *Influence without Authority.* Wiley, 2005.

Crowell, Beverly, and Beverly Kaye. "Build Your DREAM Team." *Leadership Excellence* 31, no. 4 (April 2014): 19-20.

Ensher, Ellen, and Susan Murphy. *Power Mentoring: How Successful Mentors and Proteges Get the Most Out of Their Relationships.* Jossey-Bass, 2005.

Fickenscher, Kira. "How to effectively measure mentoring programs." *TLNT—The Business of HR.* (October 2013).

Forrest, Jayson. "MENTORING MAKES IT EASY." *Money Management* (August 30, 2013): 18-19.

Frantz, Jerry. "Why advisers and mentors matter." *Smart Business Cleveland* 25, no. 10 (June 2014): 18.

Goldvarg, Damian. "THE BUILDING BLOCKS OF GREAT COACHING." *Training* 51, no. 3 (May 2014): 54-55.

Hagemann, Bonnie, and Saundra Stroope. "Bringing Your A-Game." *Personal Excellence* 19, no. 6 (June, 2014): 18-19.

Lawrence, Paul, and Ann Whyte. "Designing leadership development programs --the case for coaching." *Training & Development (1839-8561)* 39, no. 6 (December, 2012): 10-12.

Leder, Gerri. "AN ANCHOR IN STORMY SEAS." *On Wall Street* 18, no. 9 (September, 2008): 100.

Lewis, Katherine Reynolds. "5 Mentor Mistakes to Avoid." *Fortune.com. (May 2, 2014).*

Little, Kerry. "Maximising the Value of the Mentoring Process." *Charter.* (May, 2013): 26-29.

Longenecker, Clinton O. "Coaching for better results: key practices of high performance leaders." *Industrial & Commercial Training* 42, no. 1 (January, 2010): 32-40.

Meister, Jeanne C., and Karie Willyerd. "Mentoring Millennials." *The Harvard Business Review.* (May, 2010.) www.hbr.org

Messmer, Max. "Building an Effective Mentoring Program." *Strategic Finance* 84, no. 8 (February 2003): 17-18.

Michaels, Nancy. "Reinventing Win-Win-Win Business Relationships." *The Huffington Post.* (December 8, 2014).

Moore, Karl, and Sienna Zampino. "The Modern Mentor in a Millennial Workplace." *Forbes.* (September 11, 2014.) www.forbes.com

Morel, Stephen. “Onboarding Secures Talent for the Long Run.” *Workforce Management* Volume. 86, Issue 12. (June 25, 2007).

Morris, Betsy, and Natasha A. Tarpley. "So You're a Player. Do You Need a Coach?." *Fortune* 141, no. 4 (February 21, 2000): 144-154.

Patrick, Monica. “The Role of Character in Leadership.” *The Houston Chronicle.* http://smallbusiness.chron.com/role-character-leadership-31066.html.

Paul, Tony. “Bergman, remembered for marathon at-bat, dies.” *The Detroit News.* (February 2, 2015).

Perry, Phillip M. "Smart Mentoring: When Skilled Employees Share Their Knowledge." *Rural Telecommunications* 25, no. 5 (September 2006): 46-49.

Peter, Laurence J., and Raymond Hull. *The Peter Principle: Why Things Always Go Wrong.* HarperBusiness, Reprint Edition, 2011.

Rock, David, and Ruth Donde. "Driving organizational change with internal coaching programs: part one." *Industrial & Commercial Training* 40, no. 1 (January 2008): 10-18.

Rogers, Siobhan Sutherland. "Mentoring for Change: Adding value where it counts." *Training & Development (1839-8561)* 41, no. 1 (February 2014): 8-9.

Rosato, Donna. "Benefit From Being a Mentor." *Money* 42, no. 7 (August, 2013): 44.

Ross, Michael. *Overcoming the Character Deficit: How to Restore America's Greatness One Decision at a Time.* Tate Publishing, 2014.

Stachowiak, Dave. “8 Ways to Influence without Authority.” Coachingforleaders.com. (January 23, 2013).

STEER, DAN. "Onboard With It All." *T+D* 67, no. 11 (November 2013): 26-29.

Sturt, David, and Todd Nordstrom. “5 Ways People Kill Their Career Potential.” *Forbes.* (December 23, 2014). www.forbes.com.

Taie, Eman Salman. "Coaching as an Approach to Enhance Performance." *Journal For Quality & Participation* 34, no. 1 (April, 2011): 34-38.

About the author:

Ron Emery is a seasoned operations, global sourcing and supply chain professional. His focus has been on developing strategies to support business growth and cost efficiencies in a wide variety of industries. He currently serves as Director of Manufacturing and Materials for Process Technology Corporation in Mentor, Ohio and also runs his own operational consulting practice.

In his manufacturing and consulting career Ron has led several projects focused on improving operational efficiencies for many clients. Ron has a tremendous passion for operational improvement and enhancing customer relationships. Ron's passions also roll into mentoring and teaching. He has spoken at various events for ISM and APICS and teaches in the MBA programs at several universities, focusing on experiential learning and applied technologies.

Ron worked with several large international organizations, helping to identify areas for cost savings related to sourcing, procurement, logistics, distribution and operational improvement. Ron has achieved on average 20% - 45% cost reductions on major commodities and is proficient in developing global sourcing strategies while minimizing operational risks. He has started vendor management programs to shift inventory back to suppliers and has improved net payables by as much as 60%. Ron has also worked with several clients on the strategic side of their businesses with business development models and strategies such as Virtual Vertical Integration, as well as developing customer-focused supply chains. Ron has also spent much of his career outside the United States.

Ron has worked closely with companies on process improvement around material flow dealing with excess material and material management. He has served as a materials delivery manager with one of his major clients and has increased production from 60 to over 650 units per day by reducing bottlenecks and improving flow of materials to and from the production lines. He has a keen sense for process re-engineering, leading to improved efficiencies. He has also led a team from his consulting group to improve clients on time delivery performance from its suppliers from 45% to nearly 98% in a three month period. Ron has also been responsible for global fulfillment, logistics, supplier engineering and quality control. He has developed organizational strategy to create global supply chain organizations and has built global teams to support the supply chain process. He has assisted in the installation of Oracle Warehouse Management System. Ron has developed training materials to change internal cultures and instill new progressive management values within an organization. Ron is experienced in contract negotiations in all transportation modes.

Ron received his BA, Business and Economics from Hiram College in Hiram, OH and his MA, Materials Management from Antioch University in Yellow Springs, OH. Ron is a Certified Purchasing

Manager and a lifetime member of Omicron Delta Epsilon, the International Society for Economics. He also served as President of APICS Youngstown and is currently serving as Vice President. He regularly speaks at APICS/ISM events and has written his first book entitled, *"The Dysfunctional Organization-why we will never be competitive in America again."* His second book entitled *"Growing Comes from Planting Seeds—A guide to mentoring, coaching and developing business relationships*" will be published July 2015.

Made in the USA
San Bernardino, CA
28 June 2017